RACE PASSING AND AMERICAN INDIVIDUALISM

RACE|PASSING

AND AMERICAN INDIVIDUALISM

Kathleen Pfeiffer

University of Massachusetts Press
Amherst and Boston

Printed in the United States of America
LC 22002007550
ISBN 1-55849-377-8

Designed by Dennis Anderson
Set in New Baskerville
Printed and bound by Sheridan Books, Inc.

Library of Congress Cataloging-in-Publication Data
Pfeiffer, Kathleen, 1964Ö
    Race passing and American individualism / Kathleen Pfeiffer.
        p. cm.
Includes bibliographical references and index.
    ISBN 1-55849-377-8 (alk. paper)
    1.   American ìction Ñ History and criticism. 2.   Race in literature.
3.   Racially mixed people in literature. 4.   Passing (Identity) in literature. 5.   African Americans in literature.   I. Title.
    PS374.R32 P45 2003
    813.009'355Ñd c21

                                                            2002007550

British Library Cataloguing in Publication data are available.

For my colleagues, whose support and friendship
have made it a pleasure to come to work

and

for Todd and Elizabeth Estes, whose love and joyfulness
have made it a delight to return home

Contents

Introduction

IN THE NARRATIVES I examine here, mothers lie to their children, friends delude each other, wives deceive their husbands, one woman abandons her sister (helpless and alone in Grand Central Station, no less), and children betray their parents. When a light-skinned black character passes for white, it seems that social chaos erupts. The drama of passing is rich with literary possibilities: it involves mystery, betrayal, suspense, and subterfuge; it generally includes illicit sexual liaisons; and insofar as passing is predicated on the secret of one's birth and the renunciation of one's family, it relies on the promise of both revelation and reconciliation to provide a happy ending. Apart from their ability to offer exciting fodder for narrative intrigue, however, passing novels necessarily include pointed social criticism and resonant political commentary. Because motivation for passing was heightened after the Supreme Court's 1896 decision in *Plessy v. Ferguson*[1] and the subsequent enforcement of federal segregation, many passing narratives appeared in the three decades following that important legislation, and it is those novels, those characters, and those experiences that I examine here. In the late nineteenth and early twentieth centuries, an ostensible social, cultural, and familial upheaval was documented in passing narratives, and now, in the late twentieth and early twenty-first centuries, cultural and literary critics have turned considerable attention to the phenomenon.[2]

---

1. Homer Plessy, one-eighth black and visibly white, refused to sit in the Jim Crow section of an intrastate railcar and was arrested under a Louisiana law that mandated separate but equal accommodations for blacks and whites. When Judge John H. Ferguson of the Criminal Court for New Orleans ruled to uphold the state's law, Plessy appealed, alleging, among other things, that Ferguson's ruling violated his equal protection rights under the Fourteenth Amendment. By upholding racial segregation as constitutional, the *Plessy* decision allowed for the expansion of laws restricting social contact between blacks and whites.

2. See Ginsberg, ed., *Passing and the Fictions of Identity* (1996), which grew out of a Modern Language Association meeting panel on the topic and which, as Ginsberg reports, elicited an "overwhelming number of submissions" (vii). Major recent studies of passing

Passing characters literally embody the paradox of race and color because they are, by virtue of their "one drop of black blood," legally black yet visibly white. Many times, their response to this paradox defies their audience's expectations: though they may believe, on the one hand, that it is possible for blacks to aspire and succeed in America, they nevertheless decide, on the other hand, to seize their own opportunities for success by passing as white. Passing for white has long been viewed as an instance of racial self-hatred or disloyalty. It is predicated, so the argument goes, on renouncing blackness—an "authentic" identity, in favor of whiteness, an "opportunistic" one. These previous interpretations have insisted on a "racially correct" way of reading a text or a situation.[3] Such readings, however, try to categorize a character who deliberately *resists* categories. Must the passers' embrace of the potential for success to which their white skin avails them be seen simply as their co-optation by a culture founded on "white" values? Must passing necessarily indicate a denial of "blackness," or racial self-hatred and nothing more? In this book I propose that when we look at the passer as a figure who values individualism, who may be idiosyncratic, self-determining, or inclined toward improvisation, we invite a much richer and more complex reading. Moreover, when we recognize that the passer often demonstrates ambivalence about whiteness as well as blackness, we avail ourselves of the passing figure's more complicated nuances. Understood in this light, passing offers a problematic but potentially legitimate expression of American individualism, one that resists segregation's one-drop logic and thereby undermines America's consciously constructed ideology of racial difference.

Without a doubt, the novel of passing implicitly critiques the racialist presumption that equates racial blackness with textual blankness. The authors, figures, and texts examined here address the question posed by Henry Louis Gates Jr.: "how can the black subject posit a full and sufficient self in a language in which blackness is a sign of absence?"

---

include Gubar, *Racechanges*, Caughie, *Passing and Pedagogy*, and Wald, *Crossing the Line*. In addition, Sollors, *Neither Black nor White yet Both*, devotes a substantive chapter to the issue.

3. This is evident in the most recent studies of passing cited in the previous note. For instance, even as Gayle Wald views identity as a "historically pliable and multiply articulated" fiction, her introduction clearly rejects the view that passing constitutes resistance to racial hierarchies, noting instead the "inevitable complicity of resistance" and thereby suggesting that "the 'problem' of the color line has always required that subjects produce resistance in the context of the narratives that define them" (24, 10).

("Writing" 65). At the same time, however, the passing figure often personifies Ralph Waldo Emerson's transparent eyeball, the detached observer who is nothing and sees all. Throughout the works studied here, the passing figures stand outside their own reality, just as Emerson claimed to stand outside his realm, all transcendent observers who aspire to renounce the world they are observing. Yet as Carolyn Porter's discussion of "Emerson's self-contradictory formulation" makes clear, "in moments of crisis . . . the detached contemplative observer may be forced to recognize his own participation in the reality he presumes to observe" (xii). The crises faced by those who pass thus emerge from their own unavoidable and necessary engagement in the world.

Few critics have even noted the echoes of individualism that reverberate in race passing, and none have examined those echoes as fully as I do here. Many commentators have considered the degree to which passing narratives grow out of distinctly African American traditions; but as I demonstrate, those are counterbalanced by their simultaneous reflection of intellectual traditions that have generally been defined as canonical. Many passing narratives focus on the experience of disconnect between a character's inner (supposedly black) self and his or her outer (ostensibly white) self. This sense of disconnect between interior and exterior worlds reflects a discourse of subjectivity that also frames American individualism. On returning to Concord from New York City in 1842, for instance, Emerson noted a disconcerting experience in his journals. "In New York City lately, as in cities generally," he writes, "one seems to lose all substance, and become surface in a world of surfaces. Everything is external, and I remember my hat and coat, and all my other surfaces, and nothing else" (*Journals* 6: 165). Similarly, Emerson's attention to the surface world reflects the connection between the passing character's particular concern about racial identity and a broader American mythology of the individualized self. Such a sense of dissonance between the interior and exterior worlds has long animated the American literary imagination and is present in passing narratives, where a character like James Weldon Johnson's Ex-Colored Man examines his face at length in a mirror, seeking to understand his inner self by interrogating his exterior appearance. To give another example of the literary intersection between the motifs of passing and those of canonical American literature, the attention paid to the accuracy and penetrability of surfaces that we see in Nella Larsen's 1929 *Passing* (through its preoccupation with fashion, for instance) also finds a counterpart in Wallace Stevens's 1923 poem "Of the Surface of Things," as the poet acknowledges a paradox where "the world is beyond my understanding" (57). Like Larsen, Stevens articulates confusion in the face of such paradoxes between essence and appearance. "The gold tree is blue," he writes, seeking to connect the visible world with its invisible counterpart; surely this paradigm also speaks to a racial identity based on essence rather than (countermanding) appearance (57).[4]

In aligning race passing and American individualism in this book's title, I intend to connect them, to offer them as interchangeable concepts—to suggest that we think of passing *as* American individualism and vice versa. At the same time, this work insistently interrogates the very construction of passing by challenging its participation in a rhetoric of racial identity that is strictly binary and therefore necessarily incomplete. When I speak of American individualism here, I mean to evoke the mythology that animates American notions of autonomy, self-determination, and free choice. To be sure, this is a broad and ever-changing tradition, and my intention is less concerned with pinning down a particular philosophical definition than it is with teasing out an energizing discourse. Werner Sollors proposes the concepts of *consent* and *descent* in *Beyond Ethnicity*, his analysis of the tension among competing strains of ethnic identity. "Descent language emphasizes our position as heirs, our hereditary qualities, liabilities, and entitlements," Sollors explains; "consent language stresses our abilities as mature free agents and 'architects of our fate' to choose our spouses, our destinies, and our political systems" (6). These categories, directed in Sollors's study toward a clearer explication of ethnicity, fruitfully inform the definition of racial identity that I examine here, precisely because they demonstrate the distinctions drawn between ethnic identity and racial identity. Though assimilation is hardly an uncontested component of ethnic identity, the assimilated ethnic rarely faces the kind of hostility—either within the narrative itself or in the critical discourse surrounding it—faced by the passing character. Sollors identifies the emotional appeal of American individualism and hints at the inherent contradictions that emerge when it

---

4. In fact, the connection between Larsen and Stevens was both actual and ideological, as they had a friend and mentor in common: Carl Van Vechten presented Stevens's *Harmonium* to Alfred A. Knopf in 1923; he presented *Passing* to the publisher six years later.

is embraced by someone whose heredity brings not privilege but race: "America is a country which, from the times of Cotton Mather to the present, has placed great emphasis on consent at the expense of descent definitions. The widely shared public bias against hereditary privilege . . . has strongly favored *achieved* rather than *ascribed* identity, and supported 'self-determination' and 'independence' from ancestral, parental, and external definitions" (37). This celebration of achievement and independence, the sense of unlimited possibility that characterizes the "rags to riches" mythology—this consent-based structure of value—undergirds my references here to individualism.

Sollors turns a critical eye to the biracial figure in his study of interracial literature *Neither Black nor White yet Both,* and his analysis of passing frames this conflict between one's achieved and one's ascribed identity explicitly in terms of its historical and social context. "The paradoxical coexistence of the cult of the social upstart as 'self-made man' and the permanent racial identification and moral condemnation of the racial passer as 'imposter,'" Sollors rightly notes, "constitute the frame within which the phenomenon of passing took place" (250). Passing for white, that is to say, occurred within a historically and culturally specific set of circumstances and, as I suggest later in this introduction, draws on the psychosocial vocabulary that segregation institutionalized in American culture, a vocabulary that is everywhere evident in the literature of passing. I argue, for instance, that passing both employs and resists the emotional dynamics of such racist cultural forms as blackface minstrelsy in order to undermine and condemn such racist cultural practices as lynching. Passing, Sollors astutely notes, "can thus justly be described as a social invention, as a 'fiction of law and custom' (Mark Twain) that makes one part of a person's ancestry real, essential, and defining, and other parts accidental, mask-like, and insignificant—which is strange in a republican society" (249). Strange indeed: *Race Passing and American Individualism* offers a strategy for disentangling the passing character from that social fiction, for interrogating the attitudes toward selfhood that emerge, and for examining the presumptions about racial authenticity that are left behind.

The very ability to pass for white reveals the instability of race as a signifying category, an instability that legalized mandates for segregation exacerbated rather than contained. The artificiality of racial distinctions continually animates novels about passing. Pamela Caughie notes the "double logic" involved in the nomenclature of passing, which is a concept that implies a misrepresentation of oneself (179). Caughie's bold and progressive argument proposes that "all subjectivity is passing" (2), and she examines both creative and cultural sites of conflict within which various kinds of passing take place. In this way, the theoretical framework of her *Passing and Pedagogy* in part echoes Sollors's analysis of descent-based structures of identity, as Caughie asserts that "passing is also one of the practices through which we try to refuse the identities that have been historically offered to us and that continue to structure our responses even or especially when we seek to move out of them" (5). One can clearly feel the urgings of self-reliant individualism in this wish to move out of a historically defined identity and into a freer and fuller expression of selfhood.

The theoretical framework provided in the studies by Sollors and Caughie informs my argument, and I repeatedly resist the premise used in other contemporary studies of passing that accept the parameters of the term and presume that one is, in fact, "passing" for something one is not. My treatment of passing differs considerably from Gayle Wald's recent study *Crossing the Line*, for instance, with its chronological framework and examination of media (Wald focuses on later twentieth-century texts, including published autobiographies, film, and other testimonials) and, more important, its theoretical framework. Wald's argument presupposes "the enterprise of passing to be contradictory, self-defeating, or otherwise impracticable" and presents these narratives as texts that "ask contemporary readers to consider their own political, theoretical, or ideological interests in race as a site of identification and political or cultural investment, its fictional qualities notwithstanding" (7, 9). Recent debates over racial essentialism have called particular attention to passing narratives because these narratives manipulate the boundaries that order society, and they suggest the impossibility of locating any fixed identity.[5] Elaine K. Ginsberg's introduction to the seminal collection *Passing and the Fictions*

---

5. The animated and multifaceted discourse about whether identity (race, gender, ethnicity) is socially constructed or essential and inherent has shaped criticism of American literature—as well as American history, culture, political science, film, and intellectual history—in the past two decades. A special issue of *New Literary History* (31.4) in 2000 addressed the topic, "Is There Life after Identity Politics?" and its introduction offers a succinct overview of the debate's current configuration, one that tries to reconcile a notion of identity which is antiessentialist but still politically transformative. Walter Benn Michaels's essay, "Autobiography of an Ex-White Man," subtitled, "Why Race Is Not a Social Construction," has also advanced the debate by positing the inflammatory and fascinating argument that "we must give up the idea of race altogether" (125).

of Identity explains the "problem" of identity. "For both the process and the discourse of passing challenge the essentialism that is often the foundation of identity politics," she notes, "a challenge that may be seen as either threatening or liberating but in either instance discloses the truth that identities are not singularly true or false but multiple and contingent" (4). Gayle Wald similarly embraces the "socially dominant narrative of the color line" in order to examine "how subjects have sought to defy, rewrite, or reinterpret the scripting of racial identities" therein (5). Wald contends that "the very authority of the color line must also give rise to possibilities of racial transgression, or 'crossing the line'" (5).

Yet to argue that passing involves racial transgression requires that one not only accept a certain notion of racial difference, but also that one necessarily reinforces it. As Walter Benn Michaels has provocatively argued, "Under the one-drop rule . . . for a black person to pass for white is for that person to conceal whatever it is in his or her body that identifies her as being black. But since it is possible to pass only because that thing is already invisible, passing is therefore less a matter of hiding something than of refusing or failing to acknowledge something" ("Autobiography" 129). To be sure, the analysis of passing that I develop here calls particular attention to strains of resistance within passing narratives that arguments like Wald's have refused or failed to acknowledge. Indeed, I would argue that the passing characters themselves endorse Michaels's argument and refuse to acknowledge the primacy of invisible blood over visible skin. Angela Murray says as much in Jessie Fauset's *Plum Bun* when she replies to a friend's astonished cry, "Angela, you never told me you were coloured!" with equal astonishment. "Angela's voice was as amazed as her own: 'Tell you that I was coloured! Why of course I never told you that I was coloured! Why should I?'" (44).

Such amazement was possible in the decades following the Civil War, when clear divisions between the black and white races became increasingly important, even as the corresponding differences between black and white skin became less evident. The narratives I discuss here are products of that time, an era in which complete social, political, and cultural segregation could, in the nation's mind, maintain such racial clarity. A character in Willa Cather's *A Lost Lady* reflects on this cultural shift: "By God, Madam, I think I've lived too long! In my day the difference between a business man and a scoundrel was bigger than the difference between a white man and a nigger" (92). Yet the struggle to preserve such invisible differences as that which distinguishes a businessman from a scoundrel was often undermined by that difference's very invisibility. As these narratives show, passing for white was both an expression of the culture's anxiety about invisible differences and a contribution to it. Legal maneuvers sought to reinforce the inequality of the races, but interracial relations continued to produce biracial offspring. Contact between the two races thus continued to yield a symbolic mediation of racial difference. Metaphorically and aesthetically, the mulatto represents not only proof of interracial intimacy but also a prototype for future resolution. Ann duCille has argued persuasively that early African American writers created biracial characters (the mulatta in particular) for both rhetorical effect and political import. "Strategically it allowed [writers] to build a visual bridge or a graphic link between the white face of the mulatto and the black body of the slave," she explains, "not in an effort to cultivate an approving white opinion . . . but in an attempt to insinuate into the consciousness of white readers the humanity of a people they otherwise constructed as subhuman—beyond the pale of white comprehension" (7–8). And yet as passing narratives demonstrate time and time again, all racially mixed characters and individuals are doomed by their defiance of easy categorization.[6] They are forced to spend their lives as contingencies.

Rather than acknowledging that mulattoes symbolically blurred the distinctions between the races, U.S. laws and social customs following emancipation insisted on absolute racial demarcation, as if such certainty would regulate the now chaotic social (dis)order. States introduced segregation laws to impose barriers around racial identity, and class distinctions among blacks were effectively eradicated (Myrdal 580).[7] In 1896,

---

6. In her study of transvestitism, Marjorie Garber identifies this dynamic as a sort of "category crisis": "a failure of definitional distinction, a borderline that becomes permeable" wherein the transvestite becomes "a mechanism of displacement from one blurred boundary to another" (16). As a figure who challenges easy binarity, the transvestite shares much in common with one who passes. As such, Garber's argument is worth considering here, for passing creates the same space as transvestitism: "*a space of possibility structuring and confounding culture:* the disruptive element that intervenes, not just a category crisis of male and female, but the crisis of category itself" (17). The passing figure's stubborn resistance to easy categorization highlights the permeability of constructed distinctions separating races as well as texts.

7. Even Malcolm X has argued that segregation's collapsing of class distinctions among blacks was lasting and effective well into the twentieth century. The story has become legendary of a time when he debated a black academic: "'Brother Professor, do you know what they call a black man with a Ph.D.?' 'No. What?' came the reply, to which Malcolm answered simply: 'Nigger'" (Benston 151).

Plessy v. Ferguson made absolute racial distinctions into law. Yet instead of establishing clear, enforceable legislation and a solid social dictum, *Plessy* was, as Eric Sundquist convincingly argues, "at once a mockery of law and an enactment of its rigid adherence to divided, dual realities" (237). The Fourteenth Amendment was effectively divided by *Plessy* into separate and incomplete roles for Americans—state and national citizenship became distinct. For blacks who sought equal protection, Sundquist tells us, the Court "left equal protection . . . monstrously lodged in two bodies, neither of which had full responsibility for its legal or moral guarantee" (240). To a nation that craved certainty, *Plessy* offered the illusion of clear segregation. Yet it simultaneously invited subversion of the most dramatic sort: the number of light-skinned people passing for white best illustrates the potential for racial anarchy.

In arguing for Homer Plessy, Albion Tourgée explicitly and ironically evoked the dilemma of how to define racial identity. By identifying the "appearance of whiteness" as valuable property, Tourgée challenged the assumption that racial identity could be visually or objectively determined. Sundquist underscores the cultural anxiety that such an assumption uncovers and that biracial and light-skinned Americans force to the fore: "the spread of segregationist thought and policy made the light-skinned black an uncanny reminder that blackness both *was* and *was not* visible and whiteness both *was* and *was not* a form of property with legal significance" (249). Out of a desire for certainty in racial distinctions, *Plessy v. Ferguson,* together with a whole host of cultural attitudes and assumptions, made the question of racial segregation into a dangerous and subversive undertow. Nationwide, authentic whiteness became a psychological premium. Laura Browder explains the continuing resonance of this shift: "Race may be a construction, but color remains a visual cue; and most Americans use visual, physiological cues to make their judgments about a person's racial identity. The constructions of racial and ethnic identities have the psychological weight of reality" (9).

The increase in lynching and other racial violence underscored the protective value of white skin. "Spectacle lynchings were all about *making* racial difference in the New South," Grace Elizabeth Hale argues, "about ensuring the separation of all southern life into whiteness and blackness even as the very material things that made up southern life were rapidly changing" (203, emphasis added). Like James Weldon Johnson's Ex-Colored Man, who decides to pass for white after witnessing a horrific lynching, many passing figures were well aware of the threat of lynching, and the looming presence of the noose informs several of the narratives studied in this text. "In the nation at large, from 1889 to 1899," Joel Williamson reports, "on the average, one person was lynched every other day," creating an expansive graveyard of racial hatred (117). Lynching received the sanction of the U.S. government, both implicitly and explicitly. Implicit sanction of lynching came in the form of Woodrow Wilson's 1915 private screening of David W. Griffith's film *Birth of a Nation,* based on Thomas Dixon's venomous novel *The Clansman,* both of which celebrate mob rule and black oppression. More explicit was the political crusade of Rebecca Latimer Felton, the first woman to serve in the U.S. Senate, a servant of the people who used her position to advocate lynching "for the salvation of white women from the black beast rapist" (Williamson 129). Lynching depended on the evident differences between Felton's elevated "white women" and her reviled "black beasts" as much as it reinforced those differences.

Fascination with minstrel shows in the early nineteenth century had long nurtured in popular culture the ideology of bifurcated racialism which *Plessy* ultimately wrote into law and which lynching fueled. In minstrelsy, blackface entertainment employs the vividness of imitation blackness to draw attention away from the more subversive and prevalent imitation whiteness. Even in its pretheatrical roots, minstrelsy often reflected an anxiety regarding self-identity, a desire to define the self oppositionally. David Roediger notes, for example, that prior to the Civil War, many white mobs adopted blackface during roving attacks and holiday celebrations. Racial masquerade is a thoroughly American tradition, notably connected with the rebellion of the Boston Tea Party, where revolutionaries adopted the disguise of Indians. And blackface became a popular and integral aspect of Christmas celebrations, particularly in Philadelphia, where blackface mobs attacked black festivals: "The scenario is as fascinating as it is tragic. The chief attraction of masking . . . was that it offered a chance to 'act black' for a time. It also afforded the opportunity to move beyond gender boundaries and—in that the processions often went to elite places of entertainment and sometimes attacked municipal watchmen—to mock the respectable, middle class, orderly, and wealthy" (Roediger 105–06). In these scenes, racial disguise offered whites license for violence and rebellion. By exhibiting such hostile behavior through the medium of blackfaced racial disguises, whites projected and thereby created alternate racialized behaviors. The actual relationship between black skin and violent behavior became secondary to the perceived or projected one.

Early in American culture, blackface revelers and minstrel performers disconnected black skin from black identity. In bringing blackface disguises into theatrical minstrelsy, performers and audiences jointly translated the perceived danger of the roving mobs into the humiliating deprecation of slapstick and musical comedy. Roediger suggests that the content of the performances was, in many ways, of secondary importance to its bold cultural message: "Minstrelsy's genius was then to be able to both display and reject the 'natural self', to be able to take on blackness convincingly and to take off blackness convincingly. . . . At the same time, blackface minstrels were the first self-consciously *white* entertainers in the world. The simple physical disguise—and elaborate cultural disguise—of blacking up served to emphasize that those on the stage were really white and that whiteness really mattered" (116–17). If minstrelsy helped to create a superior (white) racial self by projecting an inferior (black) racial other, then like *Plessy*, it poised racial distinctions on jagged and ill-defined presumptions about authenticity and imitation. And, as with *Plessy*, the inherent contradictions of this racialist ideology rise to rupture the surface. For minstrelsy's foundational assumptions—that blackness can be adopted and discarded, while whiteness remains true and inherent—inadvertently deflated its intended object, by illustrating instead the artificiality of racially determined difference.

By disingenuously presenting as imitative, behavior that was actually self-created, minstrel entertainers participated in the cultural dissemination of racial misinformation. White minstrel entertainers manipulated blackness not only to amuse white audiences but to consolidate them racially. Moreover, minstrelsy employed the imitative behavior of blackface in order to reconstitute blackness *as* imitative of whiteness. For example, Robert C. Toll notes that early minstrel shows mockingly depicted the slave tradition of "jumping the broom" (47), a ritual that approximated marriage. The origins of this reflect a desire for the legitimacy of marriage, a social contract available only to whites. White entertainers thus portrayed blacks as striving to be like whites. More often, though, early minstrel shows sought to use and exploit genuine black culture, as its curiosity offered a greater entertainment value. The image of blackness created by minstrelsy dictated a racial identity to which black performers were forced to conform in late-nineteenth-century minstrel shows, even though minstrelsy was then fading. The reductive nature of minstrelsy's projected racial identity then became more pointed, as "whites were astonished at the diversity of Negroes' skin color" (Toll 38). Yet rather than reclaiming and redefining their racial identities, "black minstrels in effect added credibility to these images by making it seem that Negroes actually behaved like minstrelsy's black caricatures" (Toll 196). In the theater's competitive marketplace, audience approval dictated minstrelsy's content: though it offered black performers their sole opportunity at careers in entertainment, their freedom of expression and choice of material was severely limited.

When blackface minstrelsy posited authentic whiteness, Eric Lott argues, it also commodified racial identity. In Lott's reading of the cultural function of minstrelsy, blackface performances not only created white identity retroactively, they also engaged in a reverse reification, denying subjectivity and agency to blacks, a gesture of "relentless transformation of black characters into things" (29). Thus rendered marketable by minstrel performers, this white-produced black identity served whiteness doubly: it reinforced racial difference, through clearly delineated cultural juxtapositions, and it allowed white performers to make money from blackness. Minstrelsy creates powerful motivation for race passing: on its stage, blackness brings objectification; whiteness, agency. When minstrelsy, together with *Plessy*, posited—and when audiences, together with American culture, accepted—a reductive, stereotyped definition of black racial identity, a cultural barometer measuring authenticity and imitation became legally and socially authoritative.

To examine passing as an expression of American individualism, one necessarily confronts the degree to which segregation logic permeates our most deeply ingrained beliefs about identity, race, and America. An individual's ability to "pass for white" challenges the applicability of racial categories, yet those same racial categories are precisely what constitute the passing scene. In response to this paradox, *Race Passing and American Individualism* is structured as a series of paired readings that suggest the kind of exchange invited by passing. In the first two chapters, I examine two contemporaneous novels, Frances Ellen Watkins Harper's *Iola Leroy* and William Dean Howells's *An Imperative Duty*, which address the same issue—the conflict faced by a beautiful young woman who discovers that she's black—but which nevertheless draw starkly different conclusions.

The third and fourth chapters contrast the fictional autobiography of James Weldon Johnson's Ex-Colored Man with the actual (mostly unpublished) autobiographical essays written by Jean Toomer, who was himself regularly identified as (accused of, more often than not) passing for white. And the final chapters pair two Harlem Renaissance novels, Jessie Fauset's *Plum Bun* and Nella Larsen's *Passing*, to uncover the deep ideological contrasts that belie their ostensible thematic and ideological similarity.

Passing and American Individualism also examines the degree to which literary genres, modes, and forms work to support or resist segregation logic. The texts studied here were written between 1890 and 1929, a period that began with federal segregation and ended with the birth of modernism. In the final decade of the nineteenth century, American culture grappled with uncertainty, fluctuation, and transition, and this study begins by examining literature that reflects this fin de siècle anxiety. The differences between Harper's sentimental fiction and Howells's realism parallel the cultural extremes evident, for instance, in 1893, when the brutal financial collapse of the stock market's crash bitterly contradicted the pomp and extravagance of Chicago's Columbian Exposition. Such cultural divides defined the 1890s, and these are clearly reflected in the contrasts between the two. Harper's Iola Leroy makes a virtue of her "tragic octoroon" status: the blond-haired, blue-eyed woman embraces the black community as her own, thereby radicalizing the dominant ideology by which "one drop of black blood" defines one's racial identity. But Howells's Rhoda Aldgate is quotidian and realistic; after learning of her black lineage, she remains ultimately uninhibited by the abstract restrictions of what becomes for her an unenforceable, counterproductive, and morally defunct segregation.

The differences between Howells and Harper's novels also reflect the shift in race relations following Reconstruction. In the terms of *An Imperative Duty*, "one drop of black blood" confers little more than any other drop; yet in the terms of *Iola Leroy*, that one drop confers genuine blackness, a moral imperative, and a duty to the community. Howells's novel, in its time, was far more ideologically liberal; Harper's, far more conservative. And though Howells boldly contested the notion of—and hinted at the social construction in—any racial authenticity at all, Harper argues for indoctrinating a racial ideology for the black community to embrace, a notion of moral obligation and a racial identity that could be both black (on the inside) and white (on the outside). As a result, each novel appears to exchange the values, politics, and narrative style of the other. Kenneth Warren has also noted the inversions between the two novels: "In *An Imperative Duty*, a decision to serve the needs of unspoken black Southerners is represented as so much romantic nonsense. . . . the sentiments that appear humorous and slightly ridiculous in Howells's novel emerge not only as reasonable but as heroic in Harper's romance" (*Strangers* 66–67). *An Imperative Duty* ostensibly differs from *Iola Leroy* as much in politics as in style. Beneath their apparent and easily identifiable differences, however, a less easily identifiable parallel joins them. Both novels—and likewise, both authors—seek political representation and social recognition for black Americans.

In a strategy of radical individualism, literary characters who pass for white demonstrate the liberation available to Americans seeking self-actualization. Not strictly fiction, yet not entirely autobiographical, *The Autobiography of an Ex-Colored Man* blurs generic lines in much the same way that the Ex-Colored Man's passing blurs race lines. A textual changeling, Johnson's book is taxonomically slippery and contains its own indeterminacy, encoding the sort of disarray and ambivalence that passing evokes into its very pages; its own stubborn resistance to easy categorization demonstrates the permeability of constructed distinctions separating texts as well as races. The novel, like the ideology of segregation, incorporates fundamentally contradictory attitudes. The Ex-Colored Man exposes the degree to which this segregation logic permeates our most deeply held beliefs about identity, race, and the self-made man.

In 1894 Jean Toomer was born into the struggles to which such irreconcilable theories themselves gave birth. His literary significance (as author of *Cane*) and his historical significance (as grandson of Reconstruction politician P. B. S. Pinchback) were so intricately and unavoidably tied up in what he felt to be an arbitrarily imposed racial identity that a great deal of his personal and professional writing sought a place where he could be, as he put it, "just American" ("'Just'" 19). Indeed, Toomer's autobiographical writings, which are voluminous, sometimes contradictory, and richly detailed, often examine the question posed a century earlier by Hector St. John de Crevecoeur, the question that spawned an American literary tradition: "What, then, is the American, this new man?" (69). Toomer's unpublished typescript "Outline of the Story of the Autobiography" addresses the issue. "I again worked over my position, and formulated it with more fullness and exactitude. I wrote a poem titled 'The First American,' the idea of which was, that here in America we are in the process of forming a new race, that I was one of the first conscious members of this race" (55–56). "What was I?" he asks himself again. "I thought about it independently, and, on the basis of fact, concluded that I was neither white nor black, but simply an American" (15). His autobiographical prose insistently connects Americanness with— and identifies it through—writing and authorship.

Two Harlem Renaissance novels of passing that reveal much about the intersection of race and gender are also novels of manners, and in Jessie Fauset's *Plum Bun* and Nella Larsen's *Passing*, we meet protagonists whose individualism rails mightily against several competing demands. Both within the text and without, each author resists endorsing an identity that is circumscribed by race or gender. Thus, though the sort of "racially correct" way of reading passing narratives that I alluded to earlier does serve to empower black women's subjectivity by celebrating the African American culture that passing leaves behind, these novels of manners offer strategies for imagining that subjectivity differently. Ann duCille's provocative dissection of racial authenticity and proper womanhood challenges the long-standing critical presumption that such black southern folk traditions (as are present in the blues vernacular in particular) represent not just a genuine culture, but the sole African American cultural expression. She argues that

> such evaluations often erase the contexts and complexities of a wide range of
> African American historical experiences and replace them with a single,
> monolithic, if valorized, construction: "authentic" blacks are southern, rural,
> and sexually uninhibited. "Middle-class," when applied to black artists and
> their subjects, becomes pejorative, a sign of having mortgaged one's black aes-
> thetic to the alien conventions of the dominant culture. An era marked by the
> divergent value systems and colliding imperatives of such internally stratified
> constituencies as the black bourgeoisie, black bohemia, the working masses,
> black nationalists, the Harlem-centered literati, and the so-called Talented
> Tenth is narrowly categorized as "licentious" and sexually "sensational." (71)

In focusing her analysis primarily on black women writers and their strategies of resistance, duCille's thoughtfully nuanced argument offers observations about racial authenticity's potential to oppress. She locates authenticity, as the previous quote shows, in terms of vernacular, offering the paradigm of blues music as a frame. "However attractive and culturally affirming," duCille rightly notes, "the valorization of the vernacular has yielded what I would argue here is an inherently exclusionary literary practice that filters a wide range of complex and often contradictory impulses and energies into a single modality consisting of the blues and the folk" (69). The blues and the folk, urban and rural, black and white: such definitive segregating designations must necessarily prove reductive, in divisive gestures that my work identifies as binary logic.

In contrast to such divisive logic, the very language of passing suggests movement and evokes a notion of transition that can be temporal, physical, or spiritual.[8] Migration reflects a passage of time and space, so it comes as no surprise that fictions of passing often involve physical travel, which was fairly typical of their authors as well. James Weldon Johnson, Jessie Fauset, and Nella Larsen were all cosmopolitan, all well-traveled, all bilingual, and all of them had lived abroad. Frances E. W. Harper was decidedly peripatetic, William Dean Howells lived abroad, and Jean Toomer's youth and early adulthood were characterized by insistent relocation. Many passing protagonists reflect this explicitly—Johnson's Ex-Colored Man and Larsen's Clare Kendry both travel Europe, Howells's Rhoda Aldgate lives in Italy, and Fauset's Angela Murray lives in Paris— and implicitly, in the critical detachment that allows them to distance themselves sufficiently from the American racial landscape in order to sympathetically imagine a passing character. In Larsen's novel, cosmopolitanism indicates reliability and directs readers to trustworthy characters: one is struck by the contrast between Brian Redfield's driving ambition to settle in Brazil and Clare Kendry's extensive travel in Europe on the one hand, and Irene Redfield's explicit desire to avoid travel, new places, unfamiliar experiences on the other.

---

8. If we read passing in the tradition of the migration narrative, we again see it participating in a distinctly African American form. Farah Jasmine Griffin has analyzed how these tales "attempt to come to terms with massive dislocation," and she notes the desire for freedom, the efforts to understand an urban context, and the drama of the originating event that propel migrants and characterize their narratives. Her argument demonstrates how migrants negotiate the struggle between "ancestors"—figures characterized as vigilant and omnipresent—and the dialectically positioned "strangers," the marginal figures who straddle the divide between old and new, familiar and unfamiliar. Griffin notes, "In the tradition of migration narratives, James Weldon Johnson's *The Autobiography of an Ex-Colored Man* is the first to suggest a lynching as the cause for the protagonist's final migration" (25). Significantly, his migration also frames and is framed by his passing for white.

More often than not, the readings offered here demonstrate the complicity of literary critics in embracing certain racial ideologies and in subverting others. In the contrast between Harper and Howells, we see how the competing demands of sentimental fiction and literary realism play out in relation to race. Literary critics make much of James Weldon Johnson's ironic presentation of the Ex-Colored Man, overemphasizing the degree to which he articulates regret about passing, even as they dismiss Jean Toomer's claim to have risen above race. And to read Jessie Fauset and Nella Larsen with sympathy for their expressions of individualism is to see profound skepticism about "sisterhood." *Race Passing and American Individualism* neither offers nor purports to offer a comprehensive analysis of passing narratives throughout American literature. To be sure, many excellent tales of passing—the work of Walter White, Charles Chesnutt, and George Washington Cable, to name but a few—receive little or no mention here. Rather, this study poses a new series of questions about racial identity and national identity, and suggests strategies for a passage across the critical divide that tends to reinforce the very logic of segregation by which passing is constructed.

1 | Passing and the Sentimental Novel

THE MOST climactic scenes in Harriet Beecher Stowe's *Uncle Tom's Cabin* (1852) show heroic blacks escaping slavery by disguising their race, nationality, class, and gender. The noble George Harris successfully frees himself from a brutal master by dressing as a Spanish gentleman, after "[a] little walnut bark made [his] yellow skin a genteel brown"; his dark skin tone is then accented with hair dyed black (182). Later, in a chapter suggestively titled "Liberty," his wife Eliza, already light enough to pass for white without needing cosmetics, cuts her hair as short as a man's and assumes coarse body language so that she and George appear to be "fellow" traveling companions. Their son Harry becomes little "Harriet," a girl accompanying the benevolent Quaker, Mrs. Smyth, disguised as "her" aunt (545–47). Five years after the Harris's deliverance, Cassy dresses as a Spanish Creole lady, accompanied by Emmeline, who, as her servant, enhances her appearance as "a lady of consideration" (597). The disguises are successful and the group live out their days in Montreal, free and happy. In *Uncle Tom's Cabin*, passing clearly condemns American society as hypocritical, for it is only through passing and leaving the United States that the characters find the personal and political independence promised in the mythology of American identity. When George explains his decision to move to Africa at the novel's conclusion, he evokes nationhood, civic potential, and self-determination. "I have no wish to pass for an American, or to identify myself with them," he argues, and this critique of American racial hypocrisy cannot be overlooked (608). George, Eliza, Harry, Cassy—all highly refined, noble, moral, and intelligent characters—achieve legal freedom and personal independence by passing and, most pointedly, by leaving the United States.

In Frances E. W. Harper's *Iola Leroy* (1892), however, light-skinned characters who might benefit from passing consciously choose *not* to pass; instead, they embrace their black identities as a means to freedom. To be black in *Iola Leroy* is to be special and distinct, and it brings a moral obligation that is noble, virtuous, and representative of Christian duty. Thus, when Harry Leroy explains his decision not to pass, Robert Johnson agrees that "such masquerading as a white man" would be "treason, not only to the race, but to humanity" (203). In Harper's novel, Harry "has greater advantages as a colored man," and his work on behalf of the race contributes to "the leading nation of the earth" (219). In *Iola Leroy*, therefore, passing makes one into "a moral cripple" (266). Rejecting Dr. Gresham's marriage proposal, Iola announces, "There are barriers between us that I cannot pass" (109), and this sense of definitive boundaries structures the novel.

What I want to suggest by juxtaposing these references to passing from two important works of sentimental fiction—the brief embrace of it in *Uncle Tom's Cabin* and the extended resistance to it throughout *Iola Leroy*—is that race passing as a theme challenges more than the racial construction of one's own identity: it also highlights the vexed interchange between one's race, one's nation, and one's self. In the contrast between the two, one sees not only evidence of the experiential differences between the white author of one novel and the black author of the other, but also an evolution in the sentimental novel's engagement with the shifting constitution of racial identity between slavery and Reconstruction. Though in many ways, Frances Harper's sentimental form declares its affinity with Harriet Beecher Stowe, her influential forbear, it is, significantly, in its presentation of racial communities and a racial identity that bears a moral obligation to the race that Harper's novel departs dramatically.[1] The rejection of passing in *Iola Leroy* is a fictional strategy that endorses the segregationist's view of racial identity and strictly distinguishes black from white.

Two oft-cited points serve well to highlight the cultural import of Harriet Beecher Stowe's novel: the first is its remarkable best-seller status (the first American book, Jane Tompkins reports, to sell more than one million copies); the second is an anecdote about Abraham Lincoln. On meeting Stowe, Lincoln reportedly quipped, "So this is the little lady who

---

1. For a fuller explanation of the racialized differences between black and white women writers, see Carby, *Reconstructing Womanhood,* especially chap. 1, "'Woman's Era:' Rethinking Black Feminist Theory"; chap. 4, "'Of Lasting Service for the Race:' The Work of Frances Ellen Watkins Harper," offers a particularly detailed examination of the novel's political subtext.

made the big war." The commercial and political success of *Uncle Tom's Cabin* emerged from the novel's evocation of Christian love and redemption, but its underlying concern with national identity and the moral state of the nation affected readers as well. As Tompkins explains, the cultural work of sentimental fiction also relies on the presence of clearly defined categories: "The power of a sentimental novel to move its audience depends upon the audience's being in possession of the conceptual categories that constitute character and event. That storehouse of assumptions includes attitudes toward the family and toward social institutions; a definition of power and its relation to individual human feeling; notions of political and social equality; and above all a set of religious beliefs that organizes and sustains the rest" (126–27). Tompkins does not list racial categories here, but they clearly perform a central function in Stowe's novel, and the manipulation of racial categories is a crucial point at which Harper's novel revises Stowe's. *Iola Leroy* departs from *Uncle Tom's Cabin* in its absolute refusal to endorse the passing on which *Uncle Tom's Cabin* depends for its ultimate closure and its final moral lesson; this fact says much about the meaning of liberty for free blacks under Reconstruction and their potential to realize a fully expressed individual identity.

Frances Harper viewed her role as an artist to be an expression of political agency: insofar as the need for black America's political representation was dire in the early 1890s, her goals in composing *Iola Leroy* stood high. John Ernest notes that the novel posed "grave risks to her hard-won career as poet, orator and activist" because she risked "not only her reputation but also . . . her inevitable role as a representative of her race" (497).[2] Harper aimed for more than critical acclaim; indeed, she hoped the popular appeal of her novel would assuage the danger of racism as it expressed itself following Reconstruction. As the most violent and brutal means of expressing racial fears and enforcing segregation, the lynching condoned by Southern communities emblazoned Harper's life, work, and writing. She was an outspoken opponent of such mob rule, a tireless speaker on behalf of black civil rights, a poet whose politics often expressed themselves in verse, and a friend and ally of antilynching advocate Ida B. Wells. In writing *Iola Leroy*, Frances Harper used fiction to ad-

---

2. Ernest acknowledges his debt to Frances Smith Foster's introduction to the Schomburg Library edition of *Iola Leroy* for this point.

dress social ills—lynching, disenfranchisement, and rape all figure into the novel's plot. Moreover, Harper had few illusions about the costs of political work: she saw firsthand the conflict between white women's suffrage and that of blacks when she decided to support Frederick Douglass in 1869 as he encouraged white suffragists Susan B. Anthony and Elizabeth Cady Stanton to put race above gender in the American Equal Rights Association's discussion of the Fifteenth Amendment. "When it is a question of race we let the lesser question of sex go," Harper argued. "But the white women go all for sex, letting race occupy a minor position" (qtd. in Hale 32). As Hazel Carby evaluates the conflict, she recognizes, "Harper concluded that in this particular situation gender was not sufficient grounds for solidarity" (*Reconstructing* 68). Long before she wrote *Iola Leroy*, then, Harper understood well that the competing claims of race and gender would influence the novel's reception as surely as that same conflict informed its plot.

We ought not underestimate the social power of Harper's racial authority. In her day, Harper's authenticity as both a woman and a black was contested, and her authority was granted reluctantly. A letter written by Harper while she traveled and lectured, this time in Georgia in 1870, records the fact. "I don't know but that you would laugh if you were to hear some of the remarks my lectures call forth: 'She is a man,' again 'She is not colored, she is painted'" (qtd. in Foster 126–27). Because, in Harper's day, excellence and efficacy were equated with white male privilege, her identity as black and female confounded her audience's expectations. Her profound success as a lecturer and political activist, then, depended on her ability to contest boundaries—between black and white, male and female—and to evoke the authority of the one in order to articulate the dispossession of the other. One might say that Harper's own accomplishments depended on a particularly canny sort of passing.

Today, by contrast, Harper's racial identity, her political work, her historical significance, her position as spokeswoman for black America and especially for black women—these accomplishments grant her fiction particular status. Many of the critical evaluations of *Iola Leroy* in the past two decades point to its political value as evidence of its literary merit. Noting that the novel "was read in its own day and has never been lost either from memory or from notice," Elizabeth Ammons notes: "The signal feature of Harper's life and work, it seems to me, was her combined commitment to action and to art. She wove her poems into the countless public speeches she delivered, illustrating thereby how completely inseparable art and political activism were for her" ("Legacy" 63–64). Hazel Carby affirms the point, arguing, "*Iola Leroy* needs to be assessed not only in formal literary terms but also with close reference to its political intent, as a novel which was written to promote social change, to aid in the uplifting of the race" (*Reconstructing* 63). Clearly, Harper considered her role as an artist to be an expression of political agency, but it is worth noting that the revival of *Iola Leroy* during the past decade was also politically motivated. Paul Lauter endorses the positions of Ammons and Carby and expands the analysis of Harper's significance as a writer by considering *Iola Leroy*'s place in college classrooms. He concludes that "the issue is not whether Frances Harper is worth studying but what in our education systems makes that a question which remains to be answered" (34). In short, the current politics of curriculum decisions and of reconfiguring the American literary canon affect *Iola Leroy*'s current reception as much as post-Reconstruction's politics of racial distinctions affected its composition.

By 1892, the year Frances Harper published *Iola Leroy*, national concern for the plight of freed blacks was rapidly declining, and in the South, it was virtually nonexistent. The accomplishments of Reconstruction—not only encouraging to black Americans but necessary for their survival—had been stripped away with dizzying speed after pro–civil rights Republican governments fell in 1877. When racist Democrats "redeemed" Southern legislatures, they promptly used state power to restrict federal civil rights. And as if to underscore the reclamation of whites' local supremacy and to protest federal measures that sought to outlaw the Ku Klux Klan, the frequency of lynching rose astronomically during these years; 1892 saw a record 230 deaths, 161 black and 69 white (Zangrando 685). And these, of course, were only the *recorded* incidents. "Whites created the culture of segregation in large part to counter black success," Grace Hale explains, "to make a myth of absolute racial difference, to stop the rising" (21). In this era of profound cultural conflict, *Iola Leroy* argued for precisely the sort of rigid racial demarcations that could contain the threat of further chaos.

Harper's sentimentality may be anachronistic, but it calls attention to the awkwardness of segregation's many contradictory implications. Iola herself does not even appear in the novel's first six chapters. Instead they present, largely through dialogue, several black folk characters who subversively undermine the Confederate cause in the final weeks of the Civil War. Key among these are the light-skinned, educated Robert Johnson, who despises slavery for having taken his mother and sister away from him, and the dark, Christian, and courageous Tom Anderson, who similarly craves freedom and who seems clearly modeled on Stowe's Uncle Tom. The first time we meet blond Iola directly, she is nursing black Tom at his death bed, tenderly ministering to him—ultimately kissing his brow—after he sacrifices his life to save a boat full of soldiers. The sentimentality fosters some provocative parallels: the novel aligns past and present in its depiction of marriage, for instance. The liberal, white Northern Dr. Gresham falls in love with Iola after witnessing her devotion to Tom and, aware that she is legally black, proposes marriage. The narrative then abruptly shifts back to the time before Iola's birth when her father, Eugene Leroy, contemplated marrying his light-skinned slave Marie, Iola's mother; Leroy's selfish, racist cousin Alfred Lorraine vehemently opposes the marriage, which nevertheless takes place without his blessing. The novel's flashback continues, tracing the sheltered happy childhoods of Iola, her brother Harry, and sister Grace, none of whom know anything of their mother's racial history. In their young adulthood, Iola and Harry are sent to Northern boarding schools run by liberal white abolitionists, and while they are there, yellow fever kills their father. Alfred Lorraine then lays claim to the Leroy estate, nullifies Marie's manumission and marriage, summons Iola home, and remands Iola, Marie, and Grace to slavery, though Grace dies prostrate with grief before she can be sold. A letter from Iola allows Harry to escape Lorraine, and he joins the Union army as a black man.

Following this interjected history, the narrative returns to the Civil War, now ending, when Iola rejects Gresham's proposal. Instead of marrying, she becomes a schoolteacher to the freed slaves, then travels throughout the South, accompanied eventually by Robert Johnson, and both seek out their families. Stunning good fortune at a revival meeting not only reunites Robert with his mother but also reveals Robert to be Iola's uncle, and his mother, her grandmother. Simultaneous good fortune places Marie as a nurse in the very hospital where her son Harry recuperates from his war injuries, and a second fortuitous prayer meeting reunites the entire family. The characters engage in various civic-minded struggles for racial justice, and the novel concludes with Iola's marriage to the white-skinned, black Dr. Frank Latimer and

Harry's marriage to the brilliant, tireless, black-skinned activist Lucille Delaney.

Iola Leroy is a novel whose boldness of critique is effectively masked by sentimental Victorian propriety: Iola herself abides by the conventions of conservative society even as *Iola Leroy* the novel ridicules segregation's absurd racialist code. By embracing the segregationist logic that deemed "one drop of black blood" sufficient foundation for determining racial identity, Frances Harper's novel conspired with other cultural forces seeking to establish certainty amidst postbellum tumult. Harper's fiction offered a strategy for clarifying social and racial categories because the novel's central characters represent the population whose emergence most powerfully unsettled the social order. Grace Hale explains that educated, progressive middle-class blacks like Iola, Harry, Robert Johnson, and Dr. Latimer confounded white racism's attempts to re-create antebellum racial categories: "White efforts [in the South] to erase the visibility of middle-class blacks, to see the world as a minstrel show writ large and all African Americans as its narrow range of characters, proved more difficult. Making and perpetuating the myth of absolute racial difference in this region, the division of the world into blackness and whiteness, required the creation of racial segregation as the central metaphor of the new regional culture" (21–22). Audaciously and paradoxically, Frances Harper embraced this myth. And through its insistent rejection of passing, her novel proposed an ontological order that buttressed the segregationist's preferred social order: *Iola Leroy* embraces one-drop ideology as a moral imperative, co-opting white America's laws to black America's benefit. *Iola Leroy* has rightly been heralded as an influential contributor to the evolving attitudes about race in the United States, and its ideological efficacy depends as much on its heroine's ignorance of the fact that she had been inadvertently passing for white through her first twenty-one years as it does on her conscious decision *not* to pass through the rest of her life. "The figure of the mulatto should be understood and analyzed as a narrative device of mediation," Hazel Carby argues. "In response [to Jim Crow laws] the mulatto figure in literature became a more frequently used literary convention for an exploration and expression of what was increasingly socially proscribed" (*Reconstructing* 89). By participating in the tendency of its historical moment to establish certainty against a tide of uncertainty, however, *Iola Leroy,* like the culture of which it was a part, necessarily and simultaneously disguised and displaced moments of ambivalence, instability, and slippage. The novel's need to embrace clearly definable racial categories cannot accommodate the faulty assumption that race is a clear and stable signifying category.

Iola Leroy's insistence on absolute racial boundaries continually calls attention to the contradictions in the society and language of a segregated culture; and the mulatto characters' rejection of passing both renounces the mediation Carby cites and exacerbates segregation's disconnect between appearance and reality. Misleading appearances inform the opening chapter, "Mysteries of Market Speech and Prayer Meeting." All speech, chapter 1 warns us, deceives the unwary listener: here, the novel reveals that the seemingly benign conversations of apparently careless slaves can actually *mis*represent reality. The slaves speak in a private code of their own devising. Moreover, such a rupture in personal communication reflects a national crisis, for in Harper's fictional world, the social contract that links language to reality has been broken. The "Market Speech" is not only mysterious, it is subversive. This underground communication serves the Union's goals, and thus is linked in text and in logic to the oppressive rebel forces it seeks to undermine: "During the dark days of the Rebellion, when the bondman was turning his eyes to the American flag, and learning to hail it as an ensign of deliverance, some of the shrewder slaves, coming in contact with their masters and overhearing their conversations, invented a phraseology to convey in the most unsuspecting manner news to each other from the battlefield. . . . under this apparently careless exterior there was an undercurrent of thought which escaped the cognizance of their masters" (8–9). It is a point worth noting that Harper's rhetorical sophistication is on prominent display in this passage. The narrator explicitly employs complex formulations as if to underscore her own linguistic authority, and the passage thus demonstrates the truth of Hazel Carby's assertion that "the terrain of language is a terrain of power relations" (*Reconstructing* 17). Harper's suggestion that an "apparently careless exterior" misrepresents "an undercurrent of thought" serves to highlight the dangers at work for a white culture that prefers to view all black people, to recall Grace Hale's phrase, "as a minstrel show writ large." Hale's vocabulary is important here, for it accurately reflects the centrality of language: racial identity is, indeed, *writ* large. By thus asserting the dramatic difference between speech's true meaning and its apparent meaning, the opening pages of *Iola Leroy* textually plot the ideological dualisms that characterize the late nineteenth century's attitudes toward race.

Appearance misrepresents reality: just as Iola can be ostensibly white but essentially black, so too can market speech *seem* innocuous but actually *be* subversive. The forces unleashed by this break between appearance and reality also reveal unexpected contradictions. The internal narrative coherence in *Iola Leroy* depends on the authenticity of Iola's own "genuine" blackness; at the same time, its political success depends on white readers believing in and sympathizing with Iola's apparent whiteness. Thus, *Iola Leroy* embraces a problematically essentialist vision of race in order to promote the collective good; it reinforces "one dropism" while inverting its terms of value. The novel's opening chapter maps this inversion onto the nation's ontological and linguistic terrain. For just as choosing to engage in apparently innocuous "market speech" contributes to and supports the Union's goals, enabling its victory, so too does choosing to accept genuine blackness support national coherence and enable its self-identification. The messages encoded into market speech reflect a reality about the state of the nation that is hidden from public view. Likewise, the messages encoded into the novel's racialist ideology distinguish appearance from reality and affect the state of the nation.

By writing about the origins of Reconstruction from her own post-Redemption historical moment, Frances Harper links the chaos of the latter to its origins in the former. Several aspects of *Iola Leroy* engage this sense of rupture, displacement, or confusion. Anachronism, for instance, operates as a central trope, both within the novel and without. In situating the plot prior to the outbreak of the Civil War in order to comment on the origins of Reconstruction, Harper provides a parallel to the novel's engagement with sentimentality, for she was well aware that her publishing contemporaries, and the most popular writers of the time, were of a distinctly different school. Charles Chesnutt and Paul Laurence Dunbar had just begun to appear in print; Mark Twain, Henry James, William Dean Howells, Sarah Orne Jewett, Kate Chopin, and Hamlin Garland constitute the literary milieu of the late 1880s and early 1890s, an artistic and intellectual context that Harper ignores in favor of the melodramatic style found earlier in William Wells Brown and Harriet Beecher Stowe.

We have little reason to believe that Harper sought the critical acclaim granted her literary colleagues, however. Rather, as Hazel Carby's introduction notes, she published through a black religious press in order to reach an audience of black Sunday school children, "a contribution toward their education in the ethical and moral precepts of intellectual leadership" (xvi). Harper consciously used fiction for didactic purposes. When she explicitly states her intentions as a political agent in the note at the end of the novel, however, she seems clearly to speak to white America: "From the threads of fact and fiction I have woven a story whose mission will not be in vain if it awaken in the hearts of our countrymen a stronger sense of justice and a more Christlike humanity in behalf of those whom the fortunes of war threw, homeless, ignorant and poor, upon the threshold of a new era" (282). She proclaims the "mission" of her "story" as one that appeals to sympathy for social change, rather than to reason, moral virtue, or aesthetic value. Like the work of Harriet Beecher Stowe before her, Harper's novel relies on the political power of sentiment; her epilogue evokes the Christian sympathy that propelled Stowe's readers to political and social action in the years before the Civil War. Sentimentality works by joining feeling and action, and Harper understands this as a distinctly female force, one that works across the racial divide, and one that will join "countrymen" through their shared "Christlike humanity."

Harper's poetry was similarly painted with a sentimental palette, and it, too, explicitly cited Stowe as a literary forbear. "To Mrs. Harriet Beecher Stowe" was one of three poems Harper wrote in response to *Uncle Tom's Cabin,* and its first three stanzas begin with the emphatic repetition, "I thank thee." This poem claims Stowe as a sister, but it does so "For the sisters of our race," thereby underscoring Stowe's ability to depict race and gender as necessarily intertwined. Harper celebrates Stowe's sentimentality, and as the poet thanks the novelist for her "pleading / For the fetter'd and the dumb" we see Harper's understanding of the work's political dimension. The poet repeatedly uses metaphors for and allusions to affect, emotion, and feeling. Hearts, in particular, reappear in homage to Stowe, because her "pen of fire" has "thrilled . . . many a heart's deep lyre." But it is not only the "sisters of [the] race," who appreciate Stowe, as her "kindly words" demonstrate universal appeal. "Thou has won thyself a place," the poet asserts, "In every human heart." Stowe's own Christlike love appears in the "halo that surrounds [her] name," and Harper's final lines elevate the author with specifically

Christological evocations, as she concludes, "But thy best and brightest fame / Is the blessing of the poor" (qtd. in Foster 57).

If, as I have argued, Stowe deployed passing to highlight American racial hypocrisy, it is clear that the efficacy of *Uncle Tom's Cabin* as an agent of social change also depended on passing of a sort: its ability to merge and confuse fact and fiction. Clearly, the factual reliability of its depicted scenes contributed to its appeal. Stowe sought to underscore the historical validity of her novel and therefore published *A Key to* Uncle Tom's Cabin one year after the novel appeared in print. In *A Key*, a compilation of court records, newspaper accounts, and private letters authenticate the central plot lines of the novel. Indeed, Philip Brian Harper has argued that the efficacy of *Uncle Tom's Cabin* as an agent of social change relied on the rupture and mutability of the crucial barrier separating public and private space. The novel, he writes, "depends for its power on a demonstration of the fundamental interrelatedness of the public and private spheres—on showing that the private *is* the public" (222). The power of *Uncle Tom's Cabin*, therefore, emerges from this complex negotiation of distinctions between public and private, fact and fiction, novel and autobiography, history and ideology.

Unlike Stowe, however, Harper insisted on absolute boundaries. In *Iola Leroy*, white-skinned characters identify themselves as black, often without question or challenge, because such acceptance serves Harper's desire to present coherence and moral virtue in the black community. Whiteness, aligned with snobbish high culture, conveys absence and insignificance; blackness, aligned with speech and folk tradition, conveys substance and purpose. Yet this ideological strength proves to be a technical weakness. For in spite of its explicit acceptance of segregation's distinction between black and white, the novel reveals implicit conflict between the cultural and linguistic poles through which it distinguishes the races. Though *Iola Leroy* apparently advocates race loyalty and testifies to black America's moral coherence, the text itself undermines that objective in several crucial places.

Anachronism within the novel both problematizes Iola's origins and disrupts the narrative sequence. In *Iola Leroy*, coherence is achieved by redirecting time's arrow: chapters reorder history as nonlinear and challenge the assumption that chronology contains its own coherence. Thus, when Dr. Gresham proposes marriage, the narrative flow is interrupted, and an interjected account of Iola's family history ruptures the Civil War plot. In this way, Iola's life (and by implication, women's lives, domestic issues, and the biracial figure) merges with national history; this bisection also aligns Iola's origins with those of the war. Moreover, the Civil War (which, as a national domestic dispute, represents divorce) forms the background against which Iola's family is divided and dismantled.[3] Because the abrupt shift positions Gresham's interracial marriage proposal in relation to the Leroy's interracial marriage, the prospect of marriage and the hope of reunion links parallel plots and repetitive time lines. Though both couples (Iola-Gresham and Marie-Eugene) share the same racial composition, social standing, and moral values, the destructive results of the Leroy's union instruct Iola to reject Gresham's proposal. This juxtaposition permits Iola to rewrite history, to undo the wrongs of her family's past; she rejects the exogamy of her parents.

The parallels between the Eugene-Marie union and the prospect of an Iola-Gresham union suggest symbolically powerful comparisons. The two proposals mark the shifting of national attitudes toward race relations, personal identity, and national identity. For example, the differences between Eugene's reasons for proposing to Marie and Gresham's reasons for proposing to Iola suggest racial progression. "I was sick nigh unto death," Leroy explains, "and had it not been for Marie's care I am certain that I should have died. She followed me down to the borders of the grave, and won me back to life and health" (68). Marie's skills and devotion as a nurse save Leroy's life. His desire to marry reflects individual self-interest and gratitude: Eugene's devotion to Marie, in short, was inspired by her devotion to him. Yet the novel's second proposal scene revises the history created by the first. For Dr. Gresham becomes devoted to Iola not out of any self-interest or gratitude for her attention to him. "Iola," he tells her, "I have loved you ever since I saw your devotion to our poor, sick boys. How faithfully you, a young and gracious girl, have stood at your post and performed your duties. And now I ask, will you not permit me to clasp hand with you for life?" (60). Gresham admires her attention to the wounded black soldiers: a racially blind national interest propels him. His appreciation for the tender care she

---

3. One might even extend this link between the familial and the national by noting that both Eugene Leroy and Abraham Lincoln inadvertently but inescapably initiated familial or national separation; moreover, each died during the journey (one literal, one philosophical) to reconciliation.

ministers to the soldiers is underscored by the use of inclusive pronoun in "our boys."

Because Iola's race loyalty forbids her from marrying Gresham, however, the novel's sympathetic interests are subsumed by its need for order. Dr. Gresham's identification with the black soldiers suggests a race-blind community built on affect rather than artifice, on sympathy rather than abstract laws. When Iola refuses Gresham's hand in marriage, the novel rejects the proposition of such a community. Iola's response precludes a domesticity modeled on the acceptance of interracial marriage and a national history reconciled to integration. By rejecting Gresham's proposal, Iola resists the offer that her mother accepted; she refuses, in a sense, to marry her father. But more specifically, she rejects her father outright by explicitly denouncing the decisions that shaped his life and that created hers: Iola will not partake in the same sort of union from which she herself was born. As Michele Birnbaum shrewdly argues, "the historical terms of marriage themselves are also refused. The 'peculiar institution' is represented as continuous with the 'holiest institution'" (13). The overlapping narratives of the two marriage proposals may critique the construction of race and gender through slavery and marriage as Birnbaum suggests, but they also cause the novel to define progress through conservatism.

Harper's rigid application of a clear racial order invariably lapses, however. The dissonance between the novel's form and its function can be seen in Harper's awkward use of dialogue for nondialogic or nonconversational purposes. "Although the narrative presence of the folk was seriously weakened by Harper's flawed attempts to render dialect through direct speech," Hazel Carby observes, "she was aware of the relationship between social power and the power of language" (*Reconstructing* 81). Yet such moments of awkwardness do more than unsettle the novel's formal structure, they also reveal social instability within the race. While *Iola Leroy* ostensibly advocates race loyalty and testifies to black America's moral coherence, the narrative itself undermines that objective in several crucial places. Against the novel's embrace of Iola as an authentic black woman, Iola's own assumptions, behavior, and language undermine her reliability as a representative of her race. The instability of race as a signifying category thus intrudes in *Iola Leroy* during the very moments when Harper relies most heavily on her audience's assumptions about her heroine's racial authority.

As Carby notes, the colloquial conversations of black folk like Aunt Linda, Uncle Daniel, and Tom Anderson contrast sharply with Iola's speech. In fact, Iola's speech often sounds remarkably writerly, and her propensity to repeat the harrowing story of her trials verbatim further undermines the credibility of her speech as dialogue. At times, Iola's speech seems intended to mask some narrative void or to fill in gaps in her character's development. For example, she responds to Gresham's marriage proposal in a particularly long diatribe, which concludes:

> The intense horror and agony I felt when I was first told the story are over. Thoughts and purposes have come to me in the shadows I should never have learned in the sunshine. I am constantly rousing myself up to suffer and be strong. I intend, when this conflict is over, to cast my lot with the freed people as teacher, helper, and friend. I have passed through a fiery ordeal, but this ministry of suffering will not be in vain. I feel that my mind has matured beyond my years. I am a wonder to myself. It seems as if years had been compressed into a few short months. In telling you this, do you not, can you not, see that there is an insurmountable barrier between us? (114)

The entire passage—most of Iola's speech throughout the novel, in fact—is characterized by carefully wrought sentences more suited to written tracts than dialogue. Abrupt shifts between sentences serve the novel's interests rather than the interests of Iola's conversations. One is struck by Iola's remarkable self-confidence and her ability to characterize her suffering with such insightful perspective even while still in the midst of it. This dialogue, in fact, seeks primarily to serve plot and character and operates only incidentally as dialogue.

Iola Leroy is a strikingly ideological book that relies heavily on dialogue to convey both the narration and the message. Dialogue, in fact, helps construct the book's ideology: it conveys Harper's heavy-handed, moralizing presence while enacting and authorizing a democracy of voices. The personal histories of characters, the scenery and climate, and the twists of plot are all framed in the spoken words of numerous characters. Hazel Carby has noted that many times, characters' speaking voices often articulate oratories given by Harper during the course of her long career. This is most clear in chapter 26, where Southern racism is given voice and challenged through the conversation of Dr. Latrobe, Rev. Carmicle, and Dr. Latimer. "The structure of this dialogue closely followed the structure of Harper's public lectures," Carby explains, "in which she would cite a prevailing Southern viewpoint and then gradually dismantle it" (*Reconstructing* 85). The proposed democracy of voices is thus rendered suspect by the fact of authorship, for Harper's agency is clearly a manipulative presence. In its anxious attempts to argue its points, the wrought quality of dialogue in *Iola Leroy* reveals far more than it intends.

There are moments in *Iola Leroy* when the author's attempts at ideological coercion so disrupt the text's coherence that Harper's syntax and grammar are compromised. This occurs during chapter 30, "Friends in Council," which seeks to portray the black community's capacity for intelligence, morality, political activity, social action, and patriotism. Such qualities are underscored by the paper topics that Mr. Stillman's *conversazione* comprises: "African Emigration" (a proposal that the group roundly denounces), "Patriotism," "The Education of Mothers," and "Moral Progress of Race." Yet this chapter—which reflects the novelist's most concentrated attempt to positively portray the best and brightest of the black community—also contains the novel's most confused prose. Harper writes: "The closing paper was on the 'Moral Progress of Race,' by Hon. Dugsdale. He said: 'The moral progress of the race was not all he could desire, yet he could not help feeling that, compared with other races, the outlook was not hopeless. I am sorry to see, however, that in some States there is an undue proportion of colored people in prisons'" (254). Such obfuscated writing disorients a reader and discredits a writer. In this instance, an indirect quote ("yet he could not help feeling") is presented as direct speech, so that Hon. Dugsdale appears to be talking about himself in the third person. Yet this third person abruptly shifts into a first person ("I am sorry to see") in the very next sentence. This odd passage best illustrates the tension central to *Iola Leroy* and the gap through which the novel can be most productively explicated; the curtain is pulled back to reveal the machinations of the author. For the question that arises here is the question raised in chapter 1: who is *really* speaking, and what is the speaker *really* saying? In the passage just cited, artistic verisimilitude is compromised when Harper tips her hand by inadvertently neglecting to attend to the "mask" of her character. Third person speech is revealed as artifice serving the author's interests (a political platform) rather than those of the character (artistic integrity).

Paradoxically, just as Harper's own rhetorical sophistication frames the passage describing the ostensibly obtuse "market speech" and thereby masks its genuine acuity, her rhetorical awkwardness shapes the passages where she strives to present the sophistication of her most elevated characters. That she is writing about a period in which President Andrew Johnson has lost control of his country only reinforces the novel's pervasive sense of rupture and displacement. The impossibility of definitively reconciling the country's many uncertainties—shifting barriers between the races, the uncertainty of postbellum race and class distinctions, and the national financial upheaval provoked by the uprooting of the Southern agrarian economy—is clearly reflected in the formal structure of *Iola Leroy*. Thus, while the plot explicitly renounces passing and endorses rigid racial boundaries, the numerous formal ruptures that emerge in service of that agenda reveal the structural instability of the plot's claims and thereby suggest their ideological weakness.

Iola Leroy, like Frances Harper, believes that writing novels can affect social change. And Iola, like Harper, was well aware of the obstacles that stood in the way of novel writing: "one needs both leisure and money to make a successful book," she tells Dr. Latimer, "it needs patience, perseverance, courage, and the hand of an artist to weave it into the literature of the country" (262). Iola Leroy and Frances Harper shared similar goals; the social contexts in which they were writing were also alike. The characters in *Iola Leroy* are deeply concerned about Harry's welfare while he works in the South, fearing he will be a victim of the random violence and lynch mobs that terrorized many black men. Mrs. Leroy articulates this fear: "I do wish the attention of the whole nation could be turned to the cruel barbarisms which are a national disgrace. I think the term 'bloody shirt' is one of the most heartless phrases ever invented to divert attention from cruel wrongs and dreadful outrages" (241). This background of violence provided both motivation and material for Iola as an aspiring author, and they reflect Harper's concerns as well.

Because Frances Harper and Iola Leroy both consider writing "a good, strong book" to be "something of lasting service for the race" (262), the author and heroine self-consciously mirror each other, linking authorship and racial authority. But this is an uneasy and problematic equivocation, for it raises difficult questions about the relationship of authorship to racial authority. For example, in arguing that Iola should write a book, Dr. Latimer explicitly cites her authoritative experience as a black woman as her most valuable asset. "Miss Leroy," he asserts, "out of the race must come its own thinkers and writers. Authors belonging to the white race have written good racial books, for which I am deeply grateful, but it seems to be impossible for a white man to put himself completely in our place. No man can feel the iron which enters another man's soul" (263). Readers who recall that Iola and Latimer are both described as not only fair skinned but blond haired can only wonder at the unintended but pointed irony of this speech. Considering this, the novel's propensity to congratulate these characters for choosing not to pass across the color line here seems disingenuous. Indeed, Iola and Frank seem to be passing for black, in a form of moral minstrelsy, where the apparent "whiteness" of their skin cannot possibly mask the genuine "blackness" of their souls; in *Iola Leroy*, that blackness guarantees spiritual salvation. And in Harper's ideological schematic, their racial authority is beyond reproach.[4]

Even as the novel consistently strives to underscore Iola's racial authenticity, her fundamental difference from other black folk characters reappears covertly in numerous scenes. When, following the war, Iola discusses her plans to assist racial uplift, she comments on her qualifications by remarking, "I used to be a great favorite among the colored children on my father's plantation" (145). Yet on her father's plantation, her position was as their owner's daughter; these were the days when Iola fervently defended slavery. Well after the war, as Iola refers to black folk as "my people," she continually distinguishes herself as intrinsically different. When, for example, the schoolhouse in which she begins her teaching career is burned to the ground, Iola responds "mournfully" and with "sorrowful dismay" (147). The black schoolchildren, however, "formed a procession, and, passing by the wreck of their school, sang: "'Oh, do not be discouraged / For Jesus is your friend'" (147). Throughout the novel's second half, even after Iola has embraced "her people," her former position as a slave owner's daughter frames the reference. Her visits with Aunt Linda, for example, reminds her of "the bright, sunshiny days when she used to nestle in Mam Liza's arms" (169). One must wonder how bright and sunshiny those days were for a woman in bondage.

Though *Iola Leroy* insists that apparently white characters are authentically black, the novel draws sharp distinctions between them and the dark-

---

4. Such a scene is comically reproduced in Mark Twain's *Pudd'nhead Wilson,* in which the brown-haired, fair-skinned, "black" character Roxy serves a more cynical author. Twain's response to segregation, like Howells's (as I show in chapter 2), ridicules the very ideology that Harper ostensibly embraces.

skinned "folk." Many times, the educated, privileged light characters instruct the darker ones to abandon their folk traditions. Robert Johnson is constantly chastising Aunt Linda, correcting her attitudes, accusing her of disloyalty. "Oh, Aunt Linda," he chides her at one point, "don't run down your race. Leave that for the white people." She responds: "I ain't runnin' down my people. But a fool's a fool, wether he's white or black. An' I think de nigger who will spen' his hard-earned money in dese yere new grogshops is de biggest kine ob a fool, an I sticks ter dat. You know, we didn't hab all dese low places in slave times. An' what is dey fer, but to get the people's money. An' its a shame how dey do sling de licker 'bout 'lection times" (160). Ironically, Aunt Linda makes moral and character discriminations that Robert Johnson's call for racial loyalty at any cost refuses to recognize. His privileged position—educated, light-skinned, well-spoken—places his opinions in a privileged light. These scenes suggest that even the dark-skinned Aunt Linda, defined through "folk dialect" and her history as a slave, cannot be fully or truly black without making a very particular politically resonant moral conversion.

Though the political and popular success of Harper's book depended on its opposition to race mixing and its embracing of "one-drop" logic, the impossibility and impracticality of such a belief continually peek through. The novel's central metaphors fold in on themselves, exposing not their metaphorical weakness but the conceptual inconsistency of the ideas they seek to bear out. Shadow—as the novel's title illustrates—is continually juxtaposed against sunshine, calling into play such paired themes as death and life, slavery and freedom, despair and hope. Yet equating shadows with life's metaphorical darkness necessarily also relates it to black skin's literal darkness, a relationship that sharply undercuts Harper's intentions. The textual ruptures and narrative anomalies described thus far result from Harper's radicalization of "one-drop" racial ideology. *Iola Leroy* anticipates *Plessy v. Ferguson* by utilizing the letter of the law against the spirit of the law. Frances Harper's apparent conservatism thus masks an iconoclastic critique: while it professes allegiance to white America's prevalent theory about racial difference, the intensity with which *Iola Leroy* applies that theory results in an implosion of segregation logic rather than a celebration of it. The elaborate architecture required to sustain racial categories crumbles beneath the weight and contradictions of its own details; racial difference is thereby revealed to be built on a ruptured foundation.

Though the explicit appeals to racial stability in *Iola Leroy* are often undermined, the novel does, in fact, present resonant models of cultural
stability. That these models appear in moments of explicit transition
highlights their metaphorical significance, for the novel consistently provides subtle but portentous commentaries on both the state and the future of the nation through the machinations of its secondary plots, set-
tings, and backgrounds. Dr. Gresham, Aunt Linda and her family, various
townspeople, students, preachers, employers, homesteads, workplaces,
schoolrooms, institutions, even Washington, D.C., itself—all of these
background players and places infuse *Iola Leroy* and carry resounding importance. They are the foils against which Harper's ostensible thesis gives
way to its antithetical subtext. In them, we find the future.

For unlike the message presented by *Uncle Tom's Cabin*, particularly
through its rejection of passing, in *Iola Leroy*, the nation's identity is
closely connected to the meaning of freedom. All of the novel's Southern
black characters unequivocally share the Northern belief that free labor
promotes progress, in contrast to slave labor's tendency to facilitate stagnation. Free blacks in *Iola Leroy* set themselves up in husbandry, as independent yeoman farmers, choosing to plant vegetable gardens and raise
farm animals for their own consumption rather than to farm cotton
crops to support a failing Southern economy. This decision is not only an
act of rebellion against slavery, but also a form of participation in a nation of independent, self-supporting citizens. By remaining in the South
and fashioning their lives and households after a Northern philosophy,
these characters provide a symbol of national reunion that is both economically practical and philosophically healing. The success and stability of these farms is only enhanced by the Southern landscape; they com-
bine "the evidences of thrift and industry" with "beautiful flowers,
clambering vines, and rustic adornments" (153).

Moreover, these postslavery communities do not rely on their members' renunciation of their individual wills; rather, individual successes
contribute to community strength. On Gundover's plantation, the former slaves choose to divide the land rather than pursue cooperative or
sharecropping ventures. This is particularly noteworthy because it indicates a desire for economic independence and personal autonomy over
the belief that a community's fortunes rise or fall together. John Salters
explains: "Arter de war war ober I had a little money, an' I war gwine ter
rent a plantation on sheers an' git out a good stan' ob cotton. Cotton war

bringin' orful high prices den, but Lindy said to me, "Now John, you'se got a lot ob money, an' you'd better salt it down. I'd ruther lib on a little piece ob lan' ob my own dan a big piece ob somebody else's" (173). John Salters and Aunt Linda use their freedom to pursue America's promised dream: they become yeoman farmers, living the life promised by Jeffersonian democracy. *Iola Leroy* also offers the vision of a merchant community dedicated to service and provision. Robert Johnson's first appearance following the war is as the successful proprietor of a hardware store he has opened. Aunt Linda prospers after the war in the same manner she set herself apart during it—by selling cakes and pies: Her first desire after accruing some capital is to buy land. Like these two, all of the novel's free blacks seek economic independence through hard work, careful investment, and prudent living.

A sense of civic duty influences this new generation, and in *Iola Leroy*, the capacity for responsible citizenship is best expressed in Uncle Ben, the faithful son who chose to stay in slavery to comfort his mother rather than to escape. In Uncle Ben, we see an honest and dedicated progressive politician. Ben's loyalty inspired "a heap of fath" in "de people" (167); their response was to send him to congress. Government in this postbellum world takes shape in familial forms; Uncle Ben becomes a "big brother" figure. It is a point well worth noting that Uncle Ben is a product of the folk tradition and is introduced into the novel through the folk characters' dialect. Though Harper never fully mastered dialect herself, her contemporaries Charles Chesnutt and Paul Laurence Dunbar both mastered and deployed the form to excellent political and literary effect. Still, Harper clearly conveys the intimation that dialect offers rhetorical and political power when, for instance, Aunt Linda describes her delight at Ben's election: "I felt like the boy who, when somebody said he war gwine to slap off his face, said 'Yer kin slap off my face, but I'se got a big brudder, an' you can't slap off his face'" (167–68). As congressman, Ben is both powerful ("dere wid dem big men . . . lookin' just as big as any ob dem") and uncorrupted by power ("jist de same as he war wen we war boys togedder. He hadn't got de big head a bit" [168]). Both a man of the people and a man for the people, Ben's membership in congress offers a prototype for grassroots republicanism.

This vision of political, economic, and democratic progress is often literalized through physical mobility. Freedom's greatest benefit is unrestricted movement, and freed men and women in *Iola Leroy* exploit the opportunity, traveling from North to South, from cabins to prayer meetings, seeking families, homes, and movement itself. When *Iola Leroy* offers a vision of postbellum America as stability, it simultaneously proposes that freedom allows unrestricted movement. The novel's two final marriage proposals, that of Frank to Iola and of Harry to Lucille, take place while the couples are out riding. The promise of future generations begins with movement, with crossing lines, with passing of a different sort.

2 | Passing and the Rise of Realism

IN HIS INTRODUCTION to Paul Laurence Dunbar's *Lyrics of Lowly Life,* William Dean Howells argues that Dunbar's appeal resides in "reasons apart from the author's race, origin and condition" (vii). Howells explains, "I accepted [his poems] as an evidence of the essential unity of the human race, which does not think or feel black in one and white in another, but humanly in all" (viii–ix). Howells seeks not to deny the existence of racial categories but to contest their relevance. Still, he cannot elide the difficulty of sustaining this "essential unity" in a segregated culture: "Yet it appeared to me then, and it appears to me now, that there is a precious difference of temperament between the races which it would be a great pity ever to lose, and that this is best preserved and most charmingly suggested by Mr. Dunbar in those pieces of his where he studies the moods and traits of his race in its own accent of our English" (ix). The introduction to Dunbar's poetry maps out in brief the contradiction that Howells had earlier sought to resolve in detail in *An Imperative Duty* (1891): namely, how to reconcile the "precious difference of temperament between the races" with his simultaneous belief in "the essential unity of the human race." Connecting ostensibly irreconcilable tenets was not an unfamiliar project: Howells believed strongly, for instance, that his combined commitments to fiction and democracy (his progressive politics are evident in the fact that he was a founding member of the NAACP) were not only complementary but interdependent. "Realism," wrote Thomas Sergeant Perry in an earlier essay on Howells, "is the tool of the democratic spirit, the modern spirit by which truth is elicited" (683). Where Frances Harper easily admits weaving *Iola Leroy* "from threads of fact and fiction" (282), Howells finds such intermediation both politically and artistically suspect.

In *An Imperative Duty,* Howells attempts to render in fiction the beliefs explicated in his criticism. Howells's lifelong concern about fiction, truth, and authorship reflected more than an aesthetic interest: as Perry's comment indicates, Howells was concerned with fiction's relationship to democracy, its impact on national identity. In "Criticism and Fiction," written the year *An Imperative Duty* was published, Howells explains that realism means "nothing more and nothing less than the truthful treatment of material" (73). Howells believes that fiction demands "truth," and this belief joins his criticism and his fiction: "We must ask ourselves before we ask anything else, Is it true?—true to the motives, the impulses, the principles that shape the life of actual men and women?" (99) "Criticism and Fiction" insists that realism can serve democracy and art equally. By emphasizing the aesthetic value of the real over that of the ideal, Howells not only questions the art value of melodramatic, romantic fiction, he also questions its political import. He proposes that the truthful treatment of material can best serve the American public: "let fiction cease to lie about life . . . let it speak the dialect, the language of unaffected people everywhere—and there can be no doubt of an unlimited future, not only of delightfulness but of usefulness, for it" (104). In Howells's vision, the author's position affects the nation's sense of self; and though an author faces moral distinctions that constantly waver, in the modern world, truth consistently discriminates among these nuances.

Yet where Howells's agenda as a realist writer and critic may find "the essential unity of the human race" compatible with Dunbar's dialect poetry, it faced considerable—and ultimately insurmountable—obstacles in reconciling this claim to "essential unity" with Dunbar's other, more classical verse. "This relationship between essence and value," Henry Louis Gates Jr. argues, "between ethics and aesthetics, became as late as Howells's review of Dunbar's *Majors and Minors,* a correlation between a metaphysical blackness and a physical blackness" (*Figures* 22). As Gates demonstrates, Howells's critical tendency was to reify the black writer's racial identity, to turn the act of production into mere (racialized) product; Howells valued the dialect poetry to an extent that was out of proportion to the range of Dunbar's gifts and lyric style. Gates's explanation of this distortion also reveals the ill fit between Howells's criticism, his fiction, and his progressive racial politics. That is, Howells's introduction to *Lyrics of Lowly Life* bespoke a conflict between his racial ideology, his progressive politics, and his literary values that appeared elsewhere, and it bore implications that were far reaching.

Howells, whose authority as arbiter of American literary taste earned him the nickname "Dean of American Letters," similarly proffered enthusiastic endorsements of Charles Chesnutt's conjure stories, delighting not only in "the novelty of the material" but also in "the author's thorough mastery of it" (699). Yet in embracing these vernacular forms, Howells seemed not to understand their political character and their potential for subversion. Dialect, as Eric Sundquist shrewdly reminds us, "became the language of the folk trickster—both the protagonist and the author—transferred to literary narrative, and Chesnutt's use of dialect must therefore be taken in part as a subtle, self-conscious examination of his relation to both the white plantation tradition and to those black writers who may have pandered to the public taste for 'darky' language" (305). Howells missed the cynicism in Chesnutt's conjure tales, but he curiously found the realism in Chesnutt's novel *The Marrow of Tradition* to be unnecessarily "bitter" (qtd. in Bell, *Afro-American* 66).

Howells's dismissal of Dunbar's nondialect poetry ("Some of these I thought very good," he wrote of Dunbar's poems in literary English in *Lyrics of Lowly Life,* "and even more than very good, but not distinctively his contribution to the body of American poetry" [ix]) and his troubled response to *The Marrow of Tradition* (of which he wrote, "it is less simple throughout, and therefore less excellent in manner" [qtd. in Bell, *Afro-American* 66]) correspond to an attitude toward African American cultural forms that Howells articulated elsewhere. In "Criticism and Fiction," for instance, he draws the contrast between the reading tastes of the "literary elect" and the "unthinking multitude," explaining that it is possible for a thinking person to take delight in amusing pleasures that may be "puerile, primitive, savage" (110–11). It remains to the reader to reconcile these implicitly racial distinctions from Howells's concurrent—yet earnest, I would argue—advocacy of "the essential unity of the human race." The racial valances in his choice of adjectives have meaning, as the developing argument makes clear. "Once more, I say, these amusements have their place, as the circus has, and the burlesque and negro minstrelsy, and the ballet, and prestidigitation," Howells explains. "No one of these is to be despised in its place; but we had better understand that it is not the highest place, and that it is hardly an intellectual delight" (111). Howells's inability to imagine minstrelsy as offering any sort of "intellectual delight"[1] corresponds to his inclination to value

---

1. Curiously, Howells's memoir, *A Boy's Town*, which was written during the same period, also evokes the minstrel show to suggest that racial identity is both a source of entertainment and a cosmetic application. "Of course you could have negro shows," Howells

Dunbar's dialect poetry over his classical verse and to recoil from Chesnutt's "bitterness," as well as his understanding of the aesthetic potential of African American literature and the depiction of black characters. Howells's political sympathies unequivocally supported progressive racial policies and promoted civil rights, and his courageous public defense of the anarchist defendants in the Haymarket Riots[2] demonstrated his willingness to stand alone in defense of an unpopular political position; indeed, as Daniel Borus has argued, Howells "linked his fight in the Haymarket case to the struggle for literary realism" (156). Yet his troubled inability to successfully integrate such politics into a theory of fiction that would embrace a fuller and more nuanced understanding of black identity found expression not only in criticism of Dunbar and Chesnutt, but also in his knotty depiction of blackness in *An Imperative Duty*.

Ostensibly plotted as a Boston-based social drama, *An Imperative Duty* resonates with the anxieties about authorship, class, and the social work of fiction that often influence Howells's writing. The novel opens with the return to Boston of Dr. Edward Olney, a gentleman physician whose identity has recently been refashioned to emphasize his profession rather than his class due to the collapse of Union Pacific stock and his subsequent loss of fortune. Olney returns to seek clients whose nervous ailments might support him in the manner to which he is accustomed but finds Boston empty of "his" class of people, an oddly disconcerting circumstance. During one of his first nights there, he is unexpectedly summoned to treat Mrs. Caroline Meredith, whose acquaintance—along

---

writes, "and the boys often had them; but they were not much fun, and you were always getting the black on your shirt sleeves" (109). As a group, the boys trivialize blackness through the mockery of minstrelsy—a form of entertainment that they associate with animal shows. This observation about how groups of whites react to blackness is indeed perceptive; David Roediger argues that minstrelsy played a central role in consolidating a white working-class identity, so that blackness and whiteness were created together, in part through minstrelsy's metaphors. Indeed, Roediger's analysis explains minstrelsy's appeal to a group of bold and barefooted boys: "In creating a new sense of whiteness by creating a new sense of blackness, minstrel entertainers fashioned a theater in which the rough, the respectable and the rebellious among crafts workers could together find solace and even joy" (115).

2. When a bomb exploded during a worker's rally in Haymarket Square, Chicago, 1886, widespread outrage and fear emerged from the popular belief that policemen were targeted in the explosion. The inquiry that followed the Haymarket affair fueled suspicion toward socialists in particular and political radicals generally.

with that of her niece Rhoda Aldgate, to whom Olney is greatly attracted—he had made months earlier in Florence. Alone with Dr. Olney, Mrs. Meredith confesses to him that the reason for her nervous distress is a secret that she has kept from Rhoda—that the girl's grandmother was a slave, owned by Rhoda's grandfather. Because Rhoda is on the verge of an engagement to a sympathetic and devoted young minister, her Aunt Caroline feels duty-bound to apprise Rhoda—and her potential fiancé—of these circumstances. Though Olney advises Mrs. Meredith to keep her secret, she ignores his counsel and devastates Rhoda with the information. Frantic and distraught, Rhoda rushes from the hotel and spends the evening wandering through Boston's black neighborhoods, eventually arriving at a black church. Her aunt, equally distraught, inadvertently consumes an overdose of the sedative Olney had prescribed for her, accidentally killing herself. In the aftermath of Mrs. Meredith's death, Olney sends Rhoda to stay with his friend Mrs. Clara Atherton who keeps him informed about the girl's condition with enough detail to allow him to time his own seduction. He visits Rhoda often, and when she confesses her racial "secret," he responds with none of the surprise and dismay that she had reasonably expected; Olney was, in truth, repulsed when he initially learned this "secret" but had long since reconsidered and recreated his response. Indeed, Olney ridicules Rhoda's plan to move to New Orleans and work among "her people." He proposes an alternative—marriage to him—which she accepts, and at the novel's end, the two move to Rome to live.

Though Frances Harper aligns her book with the past by fashioning it after the domestic sentimental tradition, *An Imperative Duty* attends to genre through its references to the realism of George Eliot. When they first met in Florence, Mrs. Meredith and Dr. Olney had spent a great deal of time discussing Eliot's 1863 realistic novel *Romola,* as, in Mrs. Meredith's estimation, the moral dilemma of Tito (the novel's central character) mirrored hers. By evoking *Romola,* one of the least admired of Eliot's novels, Howells the novelist aligns himself with an influential literary predecessor who took a great interest in social realism, as he did.[3] Howells

---

3. It may be a point worth noting that Howells the critic expressed reservations about Eliot's execution of "the art of fiction" in "Criticism and Fiction," noting that while Eliot was "first ethical and then artistic," she "transcended" Jane Austen "in everything but the form and method most essential to art, and there fell hopelessly below her" (75).

himself not only read and admired *Romola,* but "Henry James's praise of
[Howells's 1882 novel] *A Modern Instance* as 'the Yankee Romola' raises
the further possibility that the portrait of [its character] Bartley was inspired by Tito" (Lynn 256).[4] While the reference to Eliot's work offers
symmetry and coherence to Howells's tale, as Romola's sense of duty provides a moral reference for Rhoda's (and their symmetry is underscored
rhetorically through the similarity of their names), it also points to the
world that fiction creates. These references underscore Howells's prominence and authority. Through evocations of *Romola,* readers who might
follow Howells's novels, James's criticism, and George Eliot's writing are
reminded that the author of *An Imperative Duty* is a distinct force, a manipulative presence who sets up cross-references with other fictional
works in order to establish a particular sort of fictional verisimilitude.
They are reminded of the Dean's impact and influence. The exoteric life
of *An Imperative Duty* corresponds to a tension within the text itself, a tension related not only to the authorizing of fiction but also to the irrecon-
cilability of Howells's progressive racial politics and the demands of realism, as this chapter demonstrates.

An Imperative Duty represents Howells's sole fictional engagement with
"the race question," and his discomfort with working that vexed question
into "the art of fiction" is manifested in the plot's preoccupation with passing. Like Iola Leroy, Rhoda has passed for white unknowingly throughout
her youth but on learning of her racial heritage she chooses—unlike Iola
Leroy—to pass for the remainder of her life. Rhoda represents Howells's
most sustained attempt to depict black identity, if not the black experience, fictionally, and the disconnect between identity and experience, sustained throughout the novel in the passing theme, also appears in Olney's
description of Rhoda as being masked. Here is Howellsian realism's version of "market speech," for it is in the metaphor of Rhoda's mask that *An
Imperative Duty* locates the distinction between racial appearance and reality: "Olney recalled [her profile] as a mask, and he recalled his sense of
her wearing this family face, with its somewhat tragic beauty, over a personality that was at once gentle and gay. The mask, he felt, was inherited,

---

4. Narrative gimmicks in which fictional characters appeared serially in Howells's novels were familiar to his readers: for instance, Olney's socialite friend Clara Atherton first appeared along with Bartley Hubbard in *A Modern Instance.* Such gestures reinforce the coherence of his fictional worlds.

but the character seemed to be of Miss Aldgate's own invention, and expressed itself in the sunny sparkle of her looks, and ran over with a willingness to please and to be pleased, and to consist in effect of a succession of flashing, childlike smiles, showing between her red lips teeth of the milkiest whiteness, small, even and perfect" (147). Rhoda's mask contains all of the racial inflections found in Howells's other evocations of race, and it presages the characterizations of explicitly—that is, visually—black characters who appear later in the novel. Rhoda's own "willingness to please" and her "flashing, childlike smiles" come to characterize the black servants she admires, whose "soft voices and gentle manners" strike her as "charming" and "so sweet!" (153, 172).

Michele Birnbaum's excellent analysis of racial hysteria in *An Imperative Duty* and *Iola Leroy* connects Rhoda's racial identity to Howells's theory of fiction and concludes that the mask says much about the intersection of Howells's realism and his racial politics: "Rhoda's 'tragic family mask' . . . is not so much discarded as it is troped, becoming similar to what Howells, in *The Years of My Youth,* terms the 'mask of fiction' necessary for self-realization. . . . *An Imperative Duty* is, finally, not interested in unmasking at all. Rhoda's 'classic mask' . . . is a kind of ideal racial pose, less Grecian than Southern. . . . Rhoda embodies Howells's 'national fantasy' of Reconstruction; her marriage to Olney, reconstructed as a union between North and South, recapitulates her own corporeal embrace of black and white" (15). Birnbaum's shrewd analysis highlights a central theme of passing, one that runs through many passing fictions (and one that informs Jean Toomer's racial program, as I will later show): namely, seeking to resolve racial division through national unity and thereby eliding any explicit engagement with the thornier, and more entrenched, aspects of racial identity's divisive segregation logic. For Howells, the default racial position is not nonessenced, as his celebration of "the essential unity of the human race" would suggest, but white. Rhoda's own "mask" of ostensible whiteness complements her fondness for black folk: it does not misrepresent or otherwise "veil" any essential blackness. "When Howells . . . turned directly to the fictional representation of the problem of race" in *An Imperative Duty,* Kenneth Warren explains, "his narrative resolution pointed to the incompatibility of genetic definition and the demands of social uplift" (*Strangers* 65).

Four years after Howells wrote *An Imperative Duty,* Paul Laurence Dunbar's evocative poem "We Wear the Mask" would rebuke Howells's metaphorical and philosophical depiction of racial masking in the novel. Yet in Howells's introduction to Dunbar's *Lyrics of Lowly Life* (in which "We Wear the Mask" appears), as we have seen, his failure to grasp the ironic and specifically racial critique embedded in Dunbar's mask underscores both the rebuke and the critique. While Howells commends the poet's "finely ironical perception of the negro's limitations," the poet himself celebrates numerous accomplishments that are specifically *misrepresented* by the mask. It is a point worth noting that the wearer of Dunbar's mask "grins and lies" and that the poem itself pointedly repudiates such "limitations" as Howells's introduction mentions, and that it does so with rhetorically sophisticated constructions. Dunbar's protagonist is a learned trickster figure, deploying dialect for self-protection as well as self-expression: "With torn and bleeding hearts we smile / And mouth with myriad subtleties" (167). Dunbar offers a much bleaker and far more intellectually and aesthetically sophisticated account of African American culture than Howells recognizes; Dunbar's mask points to the subversion and resistence inherent in minstrelsy and dialect, a level of political cunning lost on Howells.

The ambition that stirred Howells as he wrote *An Imperative Duty* differs dramatically from that which motivated Paul Laurence Dunbar's desire for literary recognition or Frances Harper's desire for social uplift. A product of Howells's obligation to a lucrative but demanding contract with Harper and Brothers, *An Imperative Duty* is but one of numerous hastily written novels. Under terms of the contract, the Dean's novels were published annually, following serialization in *Harper's Monthly*. Recently revisited in contemporary Howells scholarship, the book (often dismissed as a novelette or novella) was widely criticized in many initial reviews as demonstrating a vulgar attitude toward and understanding of Irish immigrants and black Americans. In fact, criticism of the story's Irish population was strong and harsh enough at the time of its serialization to compel Howells to alter their depiction before the work was published as a novel.[5] Such tension over the shifting racial status of the Irish itself helped to consolidate and fortify the ideological project of segregation, a cultural transition in which, as the title of Matthew Frye

---

5. Martha Banta laments this revision, for its result is that contemporary readers unaware of Howells's emendations fail to appreciate his intended juxtaposition of blacks against Irish ("Introduction" viii).

Jacobson's study defines it, such European immigrants possessed "whiteness of a different color."

Howells was hardly alone among realist writers in teasing out the implications of these emerging varieties of whiteness and in connecting them to the emergence of realism. Mark Twain's *Pudd'nhead Wilson* appeared in 1894, and it satirically tweaks the hypocrisy of racial segregation through Roxy, a woman whose one-sixteenth of black blood dooms her to slavery even though her fifteen-sixteenths of white blood give her fair skin and soft brown hair. Twain introduces Roxy first through her voice, as Pudd'nhead Wilson overhears her conversation through an open window, so that she is identified as black in terms of oral culture. Roxy's distinctive vernacular marks her as authentically black and thus circumscribes her social and personal potential as surely as the success of Paul Laurence Dunbar's dialect poetry curtailed the possibility that his audience would appreciate his mastery of traditional forms. Wilson is shocked when he first encounters Roxy's physical self, for her body, her physical being utterly belies the racial identity posited by her voice. Twain makes Roxy well aware of this ironic division, as her son Chambers (himself an imitation son, as the novel's stupefying complexity has it)—also white in body but "black" in voice—reminds her. "Bofe of us is imitation *white*—dat's what we is—en pow'ful good imitation too—yah-yah-yah!—we don't 'mount to noth'n as imitation *niggers*" (103).

In Twain's circus of a novel, the twinned themes of imitation and duplication are continually reversed and transposed, often maddeningly so, in the service of his critique of segregation's double standard. And the biting satirical deployment of such hypocrisy was not limited to Twain's fiction. One of Twain's oft-cited letters to Howells expresses his relief at the critic's review of *Roughing It*. "I am as uplifted and reassured by it as a mother who has given birth to a white baby when she was awfully afraid it was going to be a mulatto," he wrote (Twain-Howells Letters 1: 10–11; qtd. in Sundquist 257). Twain wrote about miscegenation audaciously, and as Eric Sundquist explains, the author's cunning manipulation also reflected his attention to its implications for fiction: "'Imitation,' in Twain's usage, has multiple ramifications. It pointed to the ironies that miscegenation introduced into any variable doctrine of equality; it governed the shadowy middle ground between nature (genetics) and nurture (environment) on which Twain staged his inquiry into the behaviors of mastery and subservience; and it defined again, the shared territory of

his narrative's own 'fiction' and the racial 'fiction' of American constitutional law and social custom" (229). Twain's sense of the hypocrisy embedded in a miscegenated society's embrace of such a racial "fiction" as
segregation represented is acute indeed. As in *An Imperative Duty*, Twain
examines the social and racial tension introduced by European immigrants when he incorporates the Italian counts Angelo and Luigi into the
panorama of social competition that characterizes Dawson's Landing in
Pudd'nhead Wilson. But in Twain's novel, the counts—twins—are noble
by birth and thereby offer stability to an aristocratic social order, rather
than threatening that order, as Boston's Irish do.

Though the serialization of *An Imperative Duty* forecasted the tension-
filled differentiation between varying strains of whiteness by juxtaposing
Rhoda's "imitation whiteness" against that of its Irish characters, the
novel's publication history drew into its orbit many of the issues it overtly
raises. Howells's proclivity to question the often competing economic
and moral implications of authorship—and, by extension, the social consequences of fiction—influences the three main characters. An uneasy
association between the author himself and each of these characters contributes to the novel's ongoing examination of authorship's relation to
racial authenticity: in Olney, a class-conscious, ambitious professional
struggles to reconcile his need for money with his desire for respectabil-
ity; in Rhoda, white skin and middle-class gentility challenge the notion
of authentic blackness even in the face of clear evidence that the conventions and laws of the day made her unequivocally black; and in Mrs.
Meredith, the "author" of the "fiction" that allows Rhoda to live her life
mistaking her racial identity dies beneath the strain of what she understands to be "truth." Behind this social drama, black servants compete
with Irish immigrants for the dubious distinction of providing superior
service to the economically privileged, and their anxious and energetic
maneuvers convey their desire for full citizenship.

National duty and American identity figure into *An Imperative Duty* in
its opening pages. Dr. Olney, on returning to Boston, is overwhelmed
with a sense of its strangeness and conflates his own alienation with his
sense of the city's foreignness. Olney feels himself embarked on "foreign
travels in his native place" and discovers the "familiar [to be] bewilder-
ingly strange" (137). As Olney attempts to reorient himself by searching
for "types," Howells offers a revision of American identity by replacing national types with class types: what Olney "had seen in Liverpool and now

saw in Boston was not the English type or the American type, but the proletarian type" (137). Insofar as class identity offers mobility that national or ethnic identity cannot, in describing a city of classes rather than one of ethnicities, Howells presents a Boston of immense possibility. But Olney is nothing like Emerson's transparent eyeball; rather, he identifies Americanness with myopic individualism, that is, solely in self-centered and personal terms. His inability to discover an American "type" corresponds to his inability to find his class of people. The true Americans, he thinks, in an effort to comfort and reacquaint himself, are all at the seashore.

Yet behind this unreliable narrator's self-serving quest for an authentic Americanness that mirrors his sense of his own Americanness, a coherent, historically conscientious American identity does, nevertheless, emerge. Though Olney is reluctant to admit that Boston's immigrant workers are authentically American, their claims to the nation do, in fact, appear. For instance, he finds "the real republican manner" among these people, as evinced by their "kindness mixed with roughness" In fact, he finds these Bostonians "neither uncivil nor unkind" (138–39). Further, the reader who recalls that the heralded founding fathers were considered outlaws in their day will recognize the irony in Olney's observation that these "adoptive citizens . . . looked so much like brigands" (138). The good doctor's preoccupation with national identity mirrors Howells's own.[6]

In considering the racialized caricatures offered in the novel, one might reasonably argue that *An Imperative Duty* eschews any complex engagement with the racial tensions it evokes, that it unproblematically accepts the sorts of stereotypes celebrated in *Uncle Tom's Cabin*. Yet the

---

6. Howells aspirations to authorship began with a decidedly patriotic assignment— early in his career, he wrote a campaign biography of Abraham Lincoln. This accomplishment was duly admired by Lincoln himself, who "twice withdrew the volume from the Library of Congress while serving as President" (Lynn 89). The biography's success is worth noting here not only for the honor paid Howells by Lincoln, but also because its aesthetic merit derived from Howells's ability to identify with the great president. Kenneth Lynn argues: "the book's evocation of the wild poetry of [Lincoln's] early life in the backwoods was largely based on his biographer's memories of growing up in Hamilton, Ohio . . . behind the book's glorification of Lincoln's efforts to educate himself stood Howells's own awareness of the self-discipline required by such efforts" (90). That he and Abraham Lincoln were both self-made men was a fact of which Howells was clearly aware; such success would deeply influence each man's sense of national duty.

novel insistently reflects Howells's regard for the complexity of racial re-lations and racial distinctions, and his acute awareness of race's socio-economic construction. Though his response to Paul Laurence Dunbar and Charles Chesnutt indicates his limitations in understanding black-ness, Howells's vexed engagement with varieties of whiteness infuse *An Imperative Duty* with intellectual and aesthetic tension. Matthew Frye Jacobson explains the context within which Howells writes: "The Euro-pean immigrants' experience was decisively shaped by their entering an arena where Europeanness—that is to say, whiteness—was among the most important possessions one could lay claim to. It was their *whiteness*, not any kind of New World magnanimity, that opened the Golden Door. And yet, for those who arrived between 1840 and 1924, New World ex-perience was also decisively stamped by their entering an arena where race was the prevailing idiom for discussing citizenship and the relative merits of a given people" (8–9). In *An Imperative Duty*, the contest over whiteness and national identity is fought fiercely, and its complexity found expression in the very stereotyped presentation of blackness pre-viously described. Minstrelsy and dialect offered familiar shorthand for depicting blackness; but Howells purposely balanced these against simi-larly crude stereotypes of Irish immigrants. Such caricatures appeared in the initial serial version, which the author amended in response to pub-lic opinion, and these lost lines place blacks and Irish in a far more com-petitive engagement than the novel suggests.

The lines, attitudes, and ideology that were edited out of the bound version are products of a distinct historical moment, one heavily influ-enced by economic factors. In the edition of the book by Twayne Pub-lishers, a footnote suggests that Olney's financial crisis, evolving as it does out of the Union Pacific collapse that sparked severe nationwide depres-sion, "would 'date' the action of the novel as the middle 1870's" (Cady fn 143). This fact not only posits Olney as a representative American, connected financially (therefore fundamentally) to his fellow citizens' fate in spite of his desire for an expatriate life, it also informs the text's historical background. To situate a tale about racial identity at this junc-ture is to call attention to the cultural reconfiguration of race in terms of class. Eric Foner's important work on Reconstruction highlights the in-tersection of the two. "Rudely disrupting visions of social harmony, the depression of the 1870's marked a major turning point in the North's ideological development," he explains. "As widespread tension between labor and capital emerged as the principal economic and political problem of the day, public discourse fractured along class lines. . . . [I]n the nation's large cities . . . older notions of equal rights and the dignity of labor gave way before a sense of the irreducible barriers separating the classes and a preoccupation with the defense of property, 'political economy,' and the economic status quo" (517). In responding to his audience's protests, Howells edited out lines from the novel's serial version that underscore anxiety regarding this social disruption. That he adapted his text at all suggests the degree to which Howells depended on the good will of his reading public at this point in his career. And while American book buyers refused to confront or accept the shifting of barriers separating races and classes, the Dean of American Letters found his own financial obligations more compelling than his ability to defend his work.

Many textual emendations soften the vituperative descriptions of Boston's Irish: Howells eliminates, for example, Rhoda's comment that "the Irish are twice as stupid as the colored people and not half as sweet" ("Imperative" 198) as well as the narrator's observation about Irish Bostonians that "the old women were strong, ugly old peasant women, often with the similar cast of features which affords the caricaturist such an unmistakable Irish physiognomy" (191). Most noteworthy, readers of the book version lose a crucial key to understanding these descriptions, themselves caricatures, because Howells also edited out a line laden with the anxiety of historical transformation. In serialized form, Olney's lamentations about the grotesque crudeness of the Irish waiters end with this conclusion: "I was thinking at dinner yesterday, how much more delicate the colored waiters used to be in their insinuations" (199). Here, Olney resists the transition from race to class, from having black servants attending to his personal needs to having white servants do so. Given that his own financial instability has recently reduced him to the necessity of practicing a profession, the barriers that separate Olney from the very servants he finds so disgusting have worn thin. Howells thus limns that otherwise invisible transition in which competing claims to whiteness position themselves against (generally reductive) depictions of blackness.

It seems ironic that in spite of its author's racially sensitive desire to create a sympathetic character in Rhoda, its "black" character, *An Imperative Duty* was widely criticized for its apparent racism. Ironic, but not altogether without cause: criticism of Howells's portrayal of Boston's black community is justified, for their presentation is simplistic, reductively physical, and wholly unappealing. Both Rhoda and Olney are repulsed by black people. And his only other noteworthy writing about race, the fond and similarly sympathetic portrayal of "Mrs. Johnson" from his *Suburban Sketches*, reinforces many of the same attitudes about race that brought *An Imperative Duty* such harsh criticism. "Mrs. Johnson" is explicitly autobiographical, and it narrates the frustrating search of Howells's wife for a servant. Notwithstanding the distinction in which Howells, by virtue of the appearance of *An Imperative Duty*, has just made his money in the book marketplace and Olney, by virtue of his necessary return to Boston, has just lost his money in the stock market, a fascinating connection between Howells and Olney emerges. "The name that, with an innocent pride in its literary and historical associations, she had written at the heads of her letters," he explains as he details her attempt to locate a servant, "was suddenly a matter of reproach to her" (16), and the Howellses' concern with their social standing thus parallels Olney's obsessive concern with his own class status. Like the fictional *An Imperative Duty*, the autobiographical "Mrs. Johnson" juxtaposes the (undesirable) Irish workers—who live in "aggressive and impudent squalor"—against the black workers whose appeal can only be described as fetishized.

As Henry B. Wonham's excellent work on Howells's depictions of race has made clear, the Dean's own ambivalence about representing selfhood and his fragmented engagement with his own psychological makeup are necessarily intertwined; and they are everywhere in evidence here. "Howells often projects his own psychological dilemmas onto the 'dark shadows' of his fiction," Wonham notes (709). In "Mrs. Johnson," depictions of race suggest a romanticization of slavery wholly at odds with the progressive racial politics Howells supported: "A Libyan longing took us, and we would have chosen, if we could, to bear a strand of grotesque beads, or a handful of brazen gauds, and traffic them for some sable maid with crisped locks, whom, uncoffling from the captive train beside the desert, we should make to do our general housework forever, through the right of lawful purchase" (18). Even when he breaks out of this reverie, he views Boston's black "young ladies" as "the black pansies and marigolds and dark-blooded dahlias among womankind" and characterizes the title character initially through "her barbaric laughter and her lawless eye" (21). My intention in drawing out these connections between Olney's racism and Howells's own apparent embrace of stereotypes is not so much to condemn Howells as a racist hypocrite whose writings about race belie his politics—though the evidence here certainly suggests as much—but rather to demonstrate the curious similarity between Olney's class consciousness and Howells's own. It is to highlight the degree to which for both Olney and Howells, the differences between having black servants and having Irish servants is personally threatening and deeply vexed.

To wit, Olney's attitudes toward race and class indicate a curious and significant sort of transference. For it is precisely those very stereotypes that Olney believes are racially driven which characterize Olney himself. And insofar as *An Imperative Duty* directs tremendous antagonism toward Boston's Irish, who signify ethnic or racial otherness, they too figure into this displacement. Prominent among Olney's complaints against Boston's black and Irish workers is the fact that they are workers; they are driven, in his estimation, by mercenary motives. Irish waiters seem vulturish as servants, imposing on his privacy and independence: "He could not put out his hand to take up a bit of bread without having a hairy paw thrust forward to anticipate his want; and he knew that his waiter considered each service of the kind worth a good deal extra, and expected to be remembered for it in our silver coinage whose unique ugliness struck Olney afresh" (139). Black servants, by comparison, seem markedly more reserved, withdrawn, demure. Yet to Olney's patrician mind, even reserve was somehow a sign of greed; he thinks of how a black servant "would have clothed his greed in such a smiling courtesy and such a childish simple-heartedness that it would have been graceful and winning" (139). For Olney, asserting his class position and social prominence depends on such denigrations, such elitist interpretations of the working class. Such denigrations, as we have seen, also inform "Mrs. Johnson."

But Olney himself is motivated by the very same mercenary sense of financial need that he takes such pains to ridicule. He returns to the United States at the book's opening because he "believed that he should begin earning money in larger sums if not sooner at home" (143) and seeks, above all, "a lucrative practice for a specialist in nervous diseases, who could be most prosperous where nervous diseases most abounded" (143). And so, like the waiter who hovers so close to his chair that Olney "felt his breath coming and going on the bald spot on his crown" (139), Olney himself hovers over Back Bay "where nervous suffering, if it were to avail him, must mainly abide" (144). Like the servants who wait anxiously for the ring of a bell, Olney rushes to get dressed at 10 P.M., because he "expected the man back at once and he wished to be ready" to attend immediately to establishing his client base (146).

By contrast, Olney is charmed and amused by what he views as the mock gentility in Boston's black community. He delights in the observation that "negroes, if they wished to imitate the manners of our race, wished to imitate the manners of the best of us; they wished to be like ladies and gentlemen" (141). Olney must make such elitist distinctions in order to preserve his sense of social superiority, threatened as it is by his recent financial upheaval. If blacks who try to pass as genteel indicate a desire for social mobility, Olney's sense of social instability is registered in his own attempt to pass as a British aristocrat: "His figure had not lost its youthful slimness, and it looked even formidable in its clothes of London cut; so that any fellow countryman who disliked his air of reserve might easily have passed him by on the other side, and avoided him for a confounded Englishman" (144). Olney is quick to judge blacks as social imitators because he knows himself to participate in a social masquerade as well.

Olney's deep respect for social propriety contains a similar double edge. Though he recoils in disgust from the open displays of passion in which he sees the Irish engaging on the Boston Common, finding them "simply vulgar young people, who were publicly abusing the freedom our civilization gives their youth" (141), Olney is himself unable to contain his passion for Rhoda. By the book's end, he and Rhoda sit outside in the very same manner; after she rests her head on his shoulder, "he gathered her in his arm" (233). As Kenneth Warren argues, "Although Olney no doubt hopes that his love for Rhoda is not vulgar enough for a public garden the narrative suggests that it is not quite respectable enough for an American parlor" ("Possessing" 33). Even in his attention to national identity, Olney masks his true motives from himself. Returning to the United States, for instance, constitutes what he understands—and what the title purports—to be an imperative duty. It is, in fact, making a virtue of necessity, for it also constitutes the most expedient manner in which to replenish his depleted bank account and solidify his class position: "Olney believed that he should begin making money in larger sums if not sooner at home. Besides, he recurred to that vague ideal of duty which all virtuous Americans have, and he felt that he ought, as an American, to live in America" (143). Olney's sense of duty as an American influences his sense of duty as a physician; his civic identity thus becomes conflated with his professional identity.

Indeed, *An Imperative Duty* is more than the novel's title: it is its central motif, the thematic element that links American identity to racial identity. For Rhoda, too, feels a similar sense of patriotic duty that prefigures her aspirations to race loyalty and to serving "her people." While they were in Italy, Mrs. Meredith tells Olney, "Rhoda was always homesick for America, and always eager to meet Americans. She refused all the offers that were made for her . . . and declared that she would never marry any one but an American. She was always proclaiming her patriotism, and asserting the superiority of America over every other country" (169). *An Imperative Duty* establishes Rhoda's character in terms of her patriotism; hardly a blind chauvinist, she actively participates in creating her own sense of her own nationality. She is aware, for instance, of the historical import of her country's identity. Rhoda joins the Bloomingdale sisters in sightseeing because the group wishes "to do [their] duty by Bunker Hill Monument" (171). The choice of battleground seems particularly poignant here, for it recalls the invincibility of an untrained militia against professionally equipped British troops and offers a powerful metaphor for the sort of determination that defines Rhoda's national pride.

Still, this steadfast patriotism cannot compel her to remain in the United States, and Olney's pragmatism—his realism—and his individualism effectively counter Rhoda's sense of obligation to the black community. "Oughtn't I to go down there and help them; try to educate them, and elevate them; give my life to them? Isn't it base and cowardly to desert them, and live happily apart from them" (229), Rhoda wonders, articulating a social consciousness and moral obligation that the novel has heretofore avoided. "Yes, you would have some such duty toward them, perhaps, if you had voluntarily chosen your part with them—if you had ever *consented* to be of their kind" (229), Olney counters, proffering a notion of racial identity as something one chooses, an unwavering insistence, not on the desirability of passing, but on the legitimacy of claiming that portion of her white racial makeup that she legitimately possesses. In *Pudd'nhead Wilson*, Roxy is governed by the one-sixteenth of her ancestry that gave her black blood; but in *An Imperative Duty*, Olney argues for the primacy of Rhoda's white heritage. "Begin with *me*" (229), he insists, asserting her right to claim individual happiness over what is, in the novel's moral scheme, an abstract and socially impotent devotion to the community.

In explaining the psychological process through which Rhoda's one drop of black blood "seems to authorize—for both Olney and Howells— a suspension of the moral and critical faculties that inform the realist's representation of the world" (711), Henry Wonham's sophisticated analysis of Howells and the black body examines the deeper meaning of Howells's project. Wonham argues: "Howells was himself thoroughly engaged in 'this whole matter of the individual identity,' and indeed his propagandizing efforts on behalf of literary realism might be read as a defensive stand against the fragmentation of personality, a condition he and others associated with modernity" (712). While Howells attempts to renounce the segregation logic that defines Rhoda as black, he remains self-consciously aware of that logic's powerful cultural presence. The Dean of American Letters thus fails to use his cultural authority to any courageous or progressive effect, ultimately eliding the intersection of segregation and individualism by shipping Rhoda off to Italy. Still, *An Imperative Duty* offers a necessary counterargument to *Iola Leroy*, for the realist credo that governs Howells's fiction will not permit Rhoda to claim a black identity any more than the sentimental convention embraced by Frances Harper can allow Iola to renounce a black identity. For Howells argues in *An Imperative Duty* that appearances are not misleading: in the logic of *An Imperative Duty*, Rhoda's visible whiteness legitimately authorizes her racial whiteness. But in the process of such authorizing, the novel also discovers the impossibility of reconciling the complications of its own historical and cultural moment. In the end, patriotic Rhoda has become an expatriate; America loses its own most enthusiastic supporter.

A more progressive realism might be found, however, in the very writer whose "bitterness" Howells found so off-putting. Charles Chesnutt offered his own model citizen, "The Future American," in a series of essays by that title which appeared in the *Boston Evening Transcript* in 1900, and this prototype is an American whose multiracial heritage need not lead to an expatiate existence. Indeed, Chesnutt's opening paragraph indicts writers whose work on race "have been characterized by a conscious or unconscious evasion of some of the main elements of the problem involved in the formation of a future American race" ("American 3" 121). These essays are remarkable precisely for the boldness with which they endorse amalgamation in response to racism. Countermanding the scientific research that white supremacists used to harness in service of racial oppression, Chesnutt makes it "quite clear" that "the future American ethnic type—will be formed of a mingling, in a yet to be ascertained proportion, of the various racial varieties which make up the present population of the United States" (122).

The essay's ostentatious focus on racial mingling and blending notwithstanding, Chesnutt remained well aware of the relationship between white skin and fully vested citizenship in turn-of-the century America. "If it is only by becoming white that colored people and their children are to enjoy the rights and dignities of citizenship," he notes with ironic insight, "they will have every incentive to 'lighten the breed,' to use a current phrase, that they may claim the white man's privileges as soon as possible" ("American 1" 134). It may be precisely this irony—Chesnutt's great talent—that Howells interpreted as "bitter," and one wonders whether Chesnutt's own reference to *An Imperative Duty* as "a very pretty novel" is meant to be similarly ironic ("The Negro in Books" 433). Nevertheless, it surely *was* precisely this irony that allowed black literary expression to grow, both through and beyond the dialect traditions evident in *Iola Leroy*'s folk characters, Dunbar's shrewd poetry, and Chesnutt's wickedly subversive conjure tales. When William L. Andrews argues that "the work of Chesnutt and [James Weldon] Johnson helped preserve Afro-American realism as a literary tradition, a bridge between the antebellum and modern eras" (89), he highlights the manipulation of form at work, a sort of generic passing that is seen clearly in *The Autobiography of an Ex-Colored Man*.

3 | Passing and the Fictional Autobiography

BECAUSE THE book first appeared anonymously in 1912, *The Autobiography of an Ex-Colored Man* was, understandably, construed by its initial readers as the genuine autobiography of a light-skinned black man who had successfully passed into white society. It was, in fact, a fictional account written by James Weldon Johnson. The narrative's opening paragraphs offer contradictory motives for the document that follows: at once a divulger of secrets, a confidence man, a trickster figure, and a confessor, the Ex-Colored Man's initial self-presentation defies clear psychological categorization. Likewise, his racial liminality structures the narrative. The protagonist was born in Georgia to a former slave mother and a former slave-owning father; he and his mother move to Connecticut while he is still young. In school, the protagonist befriends not only a "big awkward boy" who is white and who he names "Red Head" (7) but also "the best scholar" who is "as black as night" and who he names "Shiny" (9). He is surprised when informed by his schoolteacher that he is himself considered black, and though many other students shun or tease him, Red Head and Shiny remain his friends, symbolically connecting him to both the white and black worlds.

The Ex-Colored Man's adolescence and young adulthood are characterized by many fluctuations and a great deal of movement. During childhood, he nurtures his interest in piano; his father visits once, and then sends him a piano, promising to "make a great man" of him (26). When the Ex-Colored Man's mother dies shortly after he graduates from high school, however, his father ignores her final correspondence, thereby abandoning his son altogether. The son gives a piano concert that successfully raises funds sufficient for his college education, but the money is stolen as he travels to Atlanta University. He takes a job in a cigar factory in Jacksonville, where he "constantly postponed and finally abandoned returning to Atlanta University" (61). After a few years in Jacksonville, he follows "a desire like a fever" and moves to New York (64), where he becomes involved in gambling, cabaret life, and ragtime music, the latter greatly capturing his interest. He also becomes involved with a wealthy white patron who pays him handsomely for his piano playing and who eventually takes him on a European tour. The Ex-Colored Man grows tired of Europe and realizes that he "should have greater chances of attracting attention as a colored composer than as a white one" (108). For this reason, he returns to the United States and travels south, engaging in many discussions about the "race question" along the way. Traveling among Southern rural black communities, the protagonist is often taken for a white man. One day in particular, he witnesses a lynching in a town where his "identity as a colored man had not yet become known" (135). The Ex-Colored Man then makes his final move, returning to New York.

Throughout the narrative, the Ex-Colored Man does not so much reject his blackness as he rejects the ontology of racial categories. When he decides to "pass" for white, this is most clear: "I finally made up my mind that I would neither disclaim the black race nor claim the white race; but that I would change my name, raise a mustache, and let the world take me for what it would; that it was not necessary to go about with a label of inferiority pasted across my forehead" (139). Because his skin is light, he is taken for white and marries a white woman, raising two children with her and achieving financial and social success. In the final two paragraphs, the Ex-Colored Man briefly expresses regret that he did not take part "in a work so glorious" as that accomplished by "that small but gallant band of colored men who are publicly fighting the cause of their race" (154). Many critics understand this regret to be a reflection of his racial self-hatred.[1]

By positioning its title character at the intersection of the white and black worlds, *The Autobiography of an Ex-Colored Man* continually challenges the binary nature of America's racial ideology. The Ex-Colored Man's continual ambivalence about whiteness and blackness reflects the implausibility of his ever being able to obtain a coherent, hegemonic racial identity. Roxanna Pisiak has suggested that his ambivalence points

---

1. Judith Berzon, for example, argues that the protagonist "trades his spontaneity, creativity, and personal and racial pride for an uneasy—and often unfulfilling—identification with white middle-class America" (159). Likewise, Valerie Smith interprets him as choosing "material security and personal safety over more precious and elusive goals," a tendency that, in her view, "leads to his ultimate renunciation of the possibility of living meaningfully as a black man" (46).

to both "the 'slipperiness' of color lines" and their relation to language and "the dichotomies of white and black words" (83). Indeed, the Ex-Colored Man insistently critiques the binary racial logic of segregation: his "autobiography" demonstrates the fundamental instability of race as a signifying category. In refusing to accept the caste status of a black man, the Ex-Colored Man rejects the rules of color division, rules that demand that one accept a position within a predetermined hierarchy. By passing for white, he turns the ruling class's assumptions about racial purity against them, infecting them with his subversive blood and exposing the ideology of "whiteness" in action. In allowing the world to accept him as white, Johnson's protagonist challenges the role of race in cultural identity. And in thematizing such passing, James Weldon Johnson proposes a psychic national unity based neither on racial opposition nor on sustaining the power of white rule, but on a mutual and collective recognition of the artificiality of racial distinctions.

Such mobility and such a need for adaptability responds to the Ex-Colored Man's historical moment. Category crisis abounded during his life span; the boundaries regulating social discourse were in violent transition, particularly in the newly emancipated South, where, significantly, the Ex-Colored Man was born and where he later returned to explore. There, the occupation and influence of federal troops and an increased presence of Northern reformers undermined previously secure notions about class, work, culture, and race. Though the troops' avowed purpose was to maintain order by imposing federal mandates, their presence inadvertently accomplished just the opposite—disorder. To free Southern blacks, the troops represented opportunity; but to many whites, they were contagion, infecting the "purity" and elegance of a formerly well-regulated Southern life.

Uncertainty faced blacks and whites both: Under slavery, intimate physical contact had been regulated, was normal and accepted. Without slavery's oppressive but clearly delineated paradigm, both races withdrew into awkward, self-imposed segregation. Normality and convention became undone. The impact of emancipation was to create a space of profound uncertainty: "unspoken" laws of behavior competed with written laws that constantly vacillated. For as surely and confidently as Reconstruction Republicans instituted enfranchisement and legal protection for free blacks during the 1860s and 1870s, Redeemer Democrats overturned these protections in the name of "home rule" and in the form of Black Codes, poll taxes, and strict segregation laws in the 1880s and 1890s.

Nationally, Northern and Southern populations blended into each other in the form of ambitious fortune-seekers: abolitionists and reformers heading south crossed paths with free blacks heading north. Many sought to relocate, taking with them cultural mores and regional idiosyncrasies, creating gaps in each region's cultural hegemony. And the explosion in railroading made transportation readily available and state lines more easily traversable. Cities and towns thus changed, their roads and boundaries and layouts evolving with the advent of streetcars. Last, men and women changed, as feminist and suffrage movements gained momentum and redefined gender discourse and social intercourse.

Politics during the Ex-Colored Man's narrative was marked by dramatic turning points, the energy behind which often arose from the region of his birth. The inconsistency and chaos of individual state legislatures in the South affected the nation as a whole, if for no other reason because emancipation and enfranchisement of former slaves greatly increased the South's congressional representation and therefore its power. In addition, politics dependent on a two-party system was challenged by a rupture resulting from the rise of Populism, a powerful grassroots political movement born of the cotton failure's agrarian depression in the 1880s and 1890s. The reliable categories provided by antebellum life having collapsed, the nation sought to create new categories through which to order itself.

Binarity continually shifted as Americans struggled to conceptualize the changes taking place. Generational conflict arose alongside industrialization: the progressive and independent youth—black and white alike—rebelled against the mores and attitudes of elders who seemed lazy or slow in an increasingly mechanized age. And as a new generation of Southern blacks looked back on past times as contemptuous, a new generation of whites began to look back on them with envy, irrevocably dislocating a space for shared experiences and mutual understanding. Antebellum oppositions, such as North/South, slave/free, and proslavery/abolitionist, which facilitated and justified both Southern rebellion and Northern aggression, had to be revised to accommodate national reunion. Invariably, conceptual specificity gave way to generalism and subjectivity: all converged on black and white.

The political and legal inconsistencies that characterized Johnson's era, as the nation struggled to compel a social evolution that would both address the shifting cultural status of blacks and mandate certainty amid rising tides of instability, contribute to the Ex-Colored Man's restlessness. Segregation is rendered suspect by his presence: his ability to pass exposes segregation laws as "legalize[d] social discrimination" from Southern whites who "had to manufacture a legal fiction" to sustain their own racial power (Myrdal 581). Like Frances Harper, Mark Twain, William Dean Howells, and Charles Chesnutt before him, in *The Autobiography of an Ex-Colored Man,* James Weldon Johnson counters that legal fiction with a literary one. That the protagonist, "by blood, by appearance, by education, and by tastes" (105) is a white man undermines the logic of *Plessy v. Ferguson.* Eric Sundquist tells us that "when he boarded a Louisiana railroad car in 1892, Homer Adolph Plessy played a deliberate role—the role, as it were, of 'imitation nigger'" (233). Like Plessy himself, the Ex-Colored Man understands the social necessity of racial role playing, and he boards many railroad cars in search of an authentic self. Both the Ex-Colored Man's restless wandering and his inconsistency of character emerge from the cultural fluctuations of the post-Reconstruction and increasingly segregated United States. Segregation's incongruities were embodied—quite literally—in citizens who, like the Ex-Colored Man, were legally black but physically white.

The setting of *The Autobiography of an Ex-Colored Man* is inscribed with these tensions of containment. When the Ex-Colored Man's restless wandering takes him from one place to another, his journeys track American race riots from Jacksonville to Atlanta to New York. And when the Ex-Colored Man sets foot in any city, ashes from blazing race riots invariably litter the streets. As the Ex-Colored Man travels the physical landscape of the United States, so does he encounter its psychological landscape. Along this terrain, where the barriers defining individual states are both invisible and definitive, the barriers defining races are likewise invisible and definitive. "There was a black country and a white country, and the frontier between them was not clearly marked and was ever shifting as if in some undeclared and usually quiet war," Joel Williamson explains. "The location and nature of the frontier were much more a function of mind than of matter, of white minds and black minds rather than white bodies and black bodies" (258). The Ex-Colored Man's embodiment of physical whiteness and legal blackness literalizes the instability of these ideological frontiers and demonstrates that their barriers are increasingly penetrable.

The Ex-Colored Man experiences both the power of whiteness and the oppression of blackness, continually traversing the barriers that seek to confine him. As a child, ignorant of his own racial status, but not ignorant about race, he helps to create the very hostile and unforgiving world that he will soon experience firsthand. He joins the white boys in tormenting the black children and calling them "niggers." He then finds himself persecuted, as these same "allies" turn on him with nasty and cruel behavior. After he is exposed, "[a] few of the white boys jeered [at him] saying: 'Oh, you're a nigger too'" (11). He cannot escape this paradox even in adulthood; by the end of the book, the Ex-Colored Man makes his living investing in real estate, perhaps in the very tenement houses where, as a black man, he was forced to live years earlier.

Throughout the narrative, we see the Ex-Colored Man repeatedly reject arbitrary classification. His lack of discipline, for example, illustrates his desire to approach learning without the confines of categories, just as his earliest memories reflect his desire to define himself individually as a musician. Early on, he demonstrates a keen interest in piano playing. Yet he resists the structure of lessons, as they "hampered" his creative ability. "My music teacher had no small difficulty at first in pinning me down to the notes" he recalls (5). The Ex-Colored Man's desire for freedom responds to the paradox created by his ambivalent racial identity. But the price he pays for this lack of discipline is seen in his ignorance of any discrimination, distinction, categories. For example, he is unable to comprehend distinctions between books, reading the Bible first as a picture book and then lumping it together with "a number of modern books" whose "authors put their best work in the first part, and grew either exhausted or careless toward the end" (16–17).

Such rebellions against convention seem, at first merely to confirm his adolescent impetuosity. Yet when considered against the narrator's pointed critique of the arbitrary historical divisions he is taught in school, his rebellion ultimately reflects the broader ideological tension in *The Autobiography of an Ex-Colored Man.* His personal "category crisis" speaks to a much larger crisis when he compares it to U.S. history: "My study of United States history had been confined to those periods which were designated in my book as 'Discovery,' 'Colonial,' 'Revolutionary,' and 'Constitutional.' I now began to study about the Civil War, but the story was told in such a condensed and skipping style that I gained from it very little real information. It is a marvel how children ever learn any history out of books of that sort" (28). Implicit in the narrator's pejorative description of such a dismembered representation of history is the supposition that imposing an inorganic structure on past events necessarily robs them of continuity, fullness, and truth. The teaching of history thus becomes as suspect as the rubrics that categorically divide it. Arbitrarily placed rubrics, he suggests, don't simply fail to teach, they blur and misrepresent history. And considering that the history of an individual life constitutes autobiography, the Ex-Colored Man's comments about the discipline of history reflect a self-consciousness about his own literary project.

Paradoxically, however, the Ex-Colored Man enters the world by cataloging it. He describes his childhood home by listing the contents of each room: "there were horse-hair-covered chairs in the parlor, and a little square piano; there was a stairway with red carpet on it leading to a half second story; there were pictures on the walls, and a few books in a glass-covered case" (4). In Europe, he looks for the arrangement that distinguishes social relations: For example, are Americans in Paris treated differently than Americans in London (99)? How are the French different temperamentally from Germans (102)? He becomes multilingual by organizing languages through "an original system of study" (96). Thus he learns Spanish, French, and German by categorization, listing, memorization. Even familial relations must, for him, be apprehended through ordering. He tries to understand his father by fitting him into some preestablished scheme: "In my mind I ran over the whole list of fathers I had become acquainted with in my reading, but I could not classify him. The thought did not cross my mind that he was different from me, and even if it had, the mystery would not thereby have been explained; for, notwithstanding my changed relations with my schoolmates, I had only a faint knowledge of prejudice and no idea at all how it ramified and affected our whole social organism" (24–25). Despite his sense that classificatory thinking misrepresents reality, the Ex-Colored Man understands his world through classification.

Yet *The Autobiography* itself repeatedly denies its readers the comforting order and neat arrangement that categorizing provides. For even as the protagonist repeatedly arranges, organizes, and systematizes, the narrative contradicts this order by defying chronology, omitting whole decades, and breaking between chapters arbitrarily. Openly rejecting convention, the novel-as-autobiography pointedly challenges

the genre distinctions on which rest our basic assumptions about literature. Though marrying and remaking genres allows Johnson to join the
imagination that fiction demands with the psychological complexity that
autobiography affords, such a tactic also reminds us that all autobiography is simultaneously ideological construction. Johnson's text mirrors the complexity of its protagonist, the one neither fiction nor autobiography, the other neither white nor black—an interdependency of
hybrids, of half-breeds, neither of which can be appropriately catego-
rized yet both of which, nevertheless, meaningfully exist.

The Ex-Colored Man continually challenges categories. Because it
permeates barriers, passing encourages multiple perspectives; conse-
quently, *The Autobiography of an Ex-Colored Man* consistently undermines
our attempts to read it through any single lens. Moments in the text that
seem to romanticize race loyalty, for instance, are often undermined
even as they're presented. For instance, when the Ex-Colored Man is
robbed during his trip to Atlanta, a black Pullman porter assists him by
loaning him money and hiding him on the train; this "generosity" con-
vinces the Ex-Colored Man that "after all there were some kind hearts in
the world" (46). The Pullman porter, however, is eventually revealed to
be the thief who robbed the Ex-Colored Man (61). Such narrative twists
puzzle readers who are invested in race loyalty and thwart one's predisposition to search the novel for racial protest. In fact, as he matures, the
Ex-Colored Man becomes so racially mobile that at times one wonders
whether he's passing for white or black. And this is precisely Johnson's
point. Having been sheltered throughout much of his childhood, the
narrator imbibes both white and black roles to a certain extent; both
roles are familiar and valued. Moreover, both identities are legitimately
his to claim.

The protagonist's sense of racial loyalty continually vacillates, calling
attention to the ambivalence with which Johnson treats passing. For example, while riding as a white on a train in the South, the Ex-Colored
Man listens in on a conversation in which a bigoted Texan spurts forth
a racist diatribe about the inferiority of blacks. In the midst of it, the
Texan fumes: "You freed the nigger and you gave him the ballot, but you
couldn't make a citizen out of him. He doesn't know what he's voting for,
and we buy him like so many hogs" (117). Many critics have long claimed
that the Ex-Colored Man's subsequent admiration of the Texan illustrates the extent of his own racial self-hatred. Robert Fleming sees this

response as highly ironic, "another indication of the fact that the main character does not feel like a member of the insulted race" (94). Marvin P. Garrett views the narrator's reaction as evidence of "the hollowness at the core of [his] moral being" (11). More recently, Gayle Wald reinforces this interpretation with her assertion that the novel "refuses to satisfy the desire for such a stabilized black masculine subject who can embody the valorous tradition" of racial uplift that is depicted in the autobiographies of Frederick Douglass and Walter White. Yet Fleming, Garrett, and Wald all presuppose—like Jim Crow laws—that the Ex-Colored Man's fundamental alliance *should* be with his "black" blood, and view it as moral failure when the protagonist feels otherwise.

The complexity of this passage, however, lies in what the critics overlook. For although the Texan does display what today seems like rank prejudice, he also reveals his concern for the valid political question of how a racially diverse society maintains political and civic responsibility among citizens. This concern ought not be undervalued, yet it often is. In addition to his concern for civic identity, the Ex-Colored Man admires in the Texan what he admires in other blacks: "they, too, defend their faults and failings. This they generally do whenever white people are concerned" (121). Neither wholly black nor wholly white, the Ex-Colored Man believes himself to be free from the politics that race loyalty demands. This allows him critical distance from such racially loyal people as those who would have him discount the Texan altogether because of his prejudice. The Texan's ability to staunchly maintain his position while recognizing that it may be indefensible ("you might convince me that you're right," he says, "but you'll never convince me that I'm wrong" [121]) reflects a tradition of rugged individualism. It is this independence, this individualism that I believe most attracts the narrator to the Texan, not his racism.

We have seen the narrator value such individualism before. In his music, the one aspect of his character that successfully mediates both his black and white personas, the protagonist asserts independence: "I have never been a really good accompanist," he tells us, "because my ideas of interpretation were too strongly individual" (19). As he matures, his independent ideas nurture his talent for music and feed his desire to succeed as an original composer. A particular fascination for translating classical music into ragtime and ragtime into classical music symbolizes the narrator's position in the world. Maurice J. O'Sullivan Jr. claims that this fascination demonstrates "a fundamental inability to accept ragtime as ragtime" (69). O'Sullivan reads this inability as "a bleaching out what is black," which he suggests occurs throughout the narrator's trials (68). But if this inclination bleaches out what is black, it also blackens what is white by simultaneously refusing to accept classical music as classical music. Many critics and readers of *The Autobiography,* like O'Sullivan, give tremendous weight to the moments when the narrator resists full participation in black culture but fail to credit the degree to which they are juxtaposed with resistance to white culture. Such blurring of musical boundaries was common at the time and helped black musicians cross over into commercially lucrative markets. It was not a one-way migration, either: "Even John Philip Sousa's band played ragtime" (Ayers 379).

That the most important moments of the narrator's white adult life take place at the piano is a fact that challenges the presumption of many critics who equate his white identity with a loss of creativity and musical expression. Valerie Smith argues that "the decision to pass for white closes off a resource from which creative expression might have sprung" (51). Joseph T. Skerrett Jr. agrees that the Ex-Colored Man's passing "has annihilated both his cultural identity and his artistic creativity" and that "his most meaningful self . . . lies withered and impotent in that little box of manuscripts" (556). And Gayle Wald condemns him for renouncing the musical tradition of his mother "for the less glorious certainty of making money" (41). But the Ex-Colored Man does not renounce music; he is, in fact, playing the piano in the scene in which he proposes to the white woman who will become his wife. "My fingers were trembling so that I ceased playing," he explains (149). Music is centrally connected to these important scenes. On proposing, he explains to her "the truth" about his legally determined racial identity, and her shock and confusion leads to a separation. In time, she returns to accept his marriage proposal, also during a scene in which the Ex-Colored Man is playing the piano. Significantly, the music he plays metaphorically underscores his rejection of binary racial categories: "I took her place at the piano and played the Nocturne in a manner that silenced the chatter of the company both in and out of the room, *involuntarily closing it with the major triad*" (152, emphasis added). The musical triad evokes the very same trinary imagery that definitive, binary racial distinctions refuse to acknowledge: this major triad in music parallels the racial triad of color and reminds us of the paradox implicit in the title of Werner Sollor's study of such characters, who are neither black nor white yet both. Rather than indicating a denial of race, therefore, the narrator's piano playing mirrors his passing: both reject binary logic by "involuntarily closing it with the major triad."

Though he laments at the book's end that he has not joined "that small but gallant band of colored men," when the Ex-Colored Man refers to his "fast yellowing manuscripts," he again evokes the paradox of race and color. Metaphorically significant, the manuscripts are yellow; their composer, by contrast is "an ordinarily successful white man" (154). Yellowing manuscripts, like the "colored men" with whom he contrasts himself, give visual evidence of their defining characteristics. These men can "publicly [fight] the cause of their race" *because* their race is publicly evident (154). But the Ex-Colored Man has no such defining characteristics, as representatives of both races have made clear. His wealthy benefactor tells him, "My boy, you are by blood, by appearance, by education and by tastes a white man" (105). Similarly, "the broadest minded colored man [he] ever talked with on the Negro question" received the Ex-Colored Man's self-identification skeptically. "In referring to the race I used the personal pronoun 'we,'" he explains. Though "his companion made no comment, nor evinced any surprise," this broad-minded man did "raise his eyebrows slightly the first time he caught the significance of the word" (110). In fact, the Ex-Colored Man is *always* taken for a white man unless he identifies himself otherwise. That his manuscripts are yellow and he, though mulatto, is white constitutes a contrast of color that underscores the paradox of race.

Because the narrator's loyalty to one race is forever tempered by his membership in another, he achieves a critical distance that allows him remarkable versatility. Early in the book, the narrator recounts a childhood habit of his in which he would substitute fantastic tales during his lessons when he couldn't understand a word or sentence: "I was prone to bring my imagination to the rescue and read from the picture," he admits (6). Such a strategy informs his reactions throughout the book, as he continually uses his own resources, rather than depending on another's interpretation, to confront an intellectual challenge or to "read" a social picture muddled by the politics of race.

Adaptability serves him well. As a child, for instance, he is just as good a white boy as he is a black one, one day throwing stones and shouting "nigger," the next day feeling instantly "the dwarfing, warping distorting influence which operates upon each and every colored man in the United States" (14). Because the protagonist can never fully understand or participate in the racial experiences of either group, he remains detached from the prejudices of race loyalty. William L. Andrews argues that such distance contributes to the destabilization of black biographical reality by endorsing Booker T. Washington's "Tuskeegeeism"—the name Andrews coins for what was accommodationism to some, realism to Washington. The Ex-Colored Man, in Andrews's view, so fully embraces Washington's realism that his final outcome also necessarily challenges it: "His breadth of experience, his criticism of whites and blacks alike, and his almost Olympian detachment from racial loyalties give him an objectivity toward the whole race question that sounds almost Tuskeegean" ("Representation" 88). His mutability, as I am arguing, becomes charged: through all of his travels, and jobs, and personas, and experiences, the Ex-Colored Man is at once every one of the people he appears to be and none of them. His only constant essential characteristic is that he has no constant essential characteristic.

Identity crisis concurs with racial indeterminacy, and so namelessness—a signal of identity crisis—abounds in *The Autobiography*. The generic mutability that results from a failure of categories—whether they seek to define race, gender, or literary form—inevitably parallels a coterminous identity crisis. Just as the noticeable absence of black skin, the mark of racial identity, highlights the breakdown of categories, so does the noticeable absence of names. It is worth paying special attention to the function of names in *The Autobiography*, for the book employs this trope to underscore its renunciation of black and white traditions. Kimberly W. Benston offers insight into the volatile nature of pronouncing, declaring, or accepting names in his thoughtful and provocative essay, "I Yam What I Am: The Topos of (Un)naming in Afro-American Literature." Arguing first that black Americans have inherited their names from "the master society," Benston then suggests that all names are "enslaving fictions" that render impossible a "truly named black self" (151). The very act of speaking a "master's" language brings with it recollections of the painful linguistic expropriation that slavery, an inescapable historical fact, can never avoid.

If, in the white or "master" tradition, the act of naming or pronouncing a name was an exercise in authority, then in the black tradition, self-rule and autonomy can only come from renouncing, from unnaming, or from renaming. By distinguishing one's self as separate from all accepted linguistic conventions, to be nameless is to derive power and authority out of a linguistic void. In this way, Malcolm X reinvented and empowered himself by rejecting his surname, a literally belittling identifier. Benston argues that renaming is an act wherein "self-creation and reformation of a fragmented familial past are endlessly interwoven: naming is inevitably genealogical revisionism" (152). All of *The Autobiography*'s characters are pointedly nameless, identified solely by their physical characteristics (Shiny, Red Head) and their roles or occupations (mother, teacher, porter, Texan). In assigning identities by withholding names, Johnson's protagonist avoids both the "master's" language and "genealogical revisionism." He avoids being co-opted by either tradition and chooses instead to create his own system of identification, one ruled neither by traditionally white class and power distinctions nor by a rebellion against that paradigm. The protagonist's own moniker announces the new order: he is not a "newly white man," but an ex-colored one, a man who refuses to recognize or submit to an order whose color consciousness is based on race.

In a world in which proper names are never used as tags of identification, nicknames and epithets then become charged with meaning. In naming Shiny, Johnson engages in the sort of wordplay that undermines our racial assumptions. Most white Americans know *Shiny* only as a diminutive epithet that can describe or address any black man. Yet within black folklore, Shine is the trickster hero whose qualities are articulated in a toast commemorating the wreck of the *Titanic*. In that tale, Shine resists the temptations of money, sex, and fame to jump overboard and then outguiles a hungry shark while swimming ashore, the shipwreck's only survivor. The trickster Shine was born into narrative during the same year as Johnson's Shiny. Johnson rewrites the folk hero Shine, too: the original trickster cares largely for self-preservation and celebrates his survival with drunkenness. Shiny, on the other hand, seeks sobriety and community. The chronological impossibility of any direct relationship between the two in no way diminishes their significant similarities: "[Shine's] abilities not only indicate an amazing physical and verbal talent but also show a capacity to turn his back on just those status symbols for which the other heroes have been fighting" (Abrahams 80). Coterminous with black folklore's evolving narrative toast, Johnson deflates the epithet by dismantling all of its assumptions, while rebuilding the folk hero into one who takes the best of both racial worlds.

James Weldon Johnson, like the Ex-Colored Man, manipulated his name in order to enhance his personal identity as an author. Names have long been the centerpiece of American mobility, and translating a foreign name into something more "American" often demonstrates civic pride and portends assimilation. Johnson was well aware of this, Eugene Levy tells us, for Johnson's name change constituted an explicit gesture of authorial self-fashioning: "The publication of *The Autobiography of an Ex-Colored Man* and the success of 'Fifty Years' encouraged Johnson to think of a literary career. To further that career he decided to drop his given middle name of William and adopt the name of Weldon. 'You can see,' he wrote George Towns, 'that Jim Bill Johnson will not do for a man who pretends to write poetry or anything else.' James Weldon Johnson, he felt, gave him a distinctive literary 'trade mark'" (146). In choosing a name so aristocratically flavored, Johnson engaged in his own assimilationist maneuvering.

Throughout *The Autobiography,* personal identity is influenced by race. When the protagonist first complains to his mother about the "niggers" at school, she scolds him harshly; "'Don't you ever use that word again,' she said" in "the first sharp word" she had ever spoken to him (10). The narrator's mother clearly understands the impact and implication of such a term and forbids him from exercising its social power. Kimberly Benston reminds us that *nigger* is a brand that seeks primarily to void "the possibility of meaning" within the black experience of selfhood (156). The narrator indiscriminately applies the term *nigger* to himself in a way that masks the fact that he is, as Langston Hughes once put it, "neither white nor black" (57). Following his scolding, the young narrator asks his mother directly if *he* is a "nigger." She responds judiciously: "'No, my darling, you are not a nigger.' She went on: 'You are as good as anybody; if anybody calls you a nigger, don't notice them.' But the more she talked, the less I was reassured, and I stopped her by asking: 'Well, mother, am I white? Are you white?' She answered tremblingly: 'No, I am not white, but you—your father is one of the greatest men in the country—the best blood of the South is in you—'" (12). The mother's attempt to reconcile the white father's physical absence with his genetic presence in the boy projects the contradiction of reifying race as blood: "The fact that the bastard had none of his parents' blood for the purpose of *inheritance,*"

Eva Saks has noted, "did not mean he had none for the purpose of *heredity*" (47). Just as anonymity—a nominal absence—becomes a forceful presence as the book reconstructs its narrator's social identity, the father's absence becomes a presence through his letters. These letters textually reconstitute a white man's obligation to his biracial child: he claims the boy as offspring and the mother as coparent, while he renounces them as family in any legal or social sense.

This passage speaks to the metaphor of the musical "major triad" because it struggles to mediate transitions between polarized dualities—from childhood to adulthood, from innocence to knowledge, from whiteness to blackness. The protagonist will never successfully make any of these transitions in his life because the intersection at which all of them meet—the question, am I white or am I nigger?—is never directly answered; moreover, the question is fundamentally unanswerable. For as the father's "absent presence" exposes the contradictions of defining race through blood for the cross-purposes of inheritance and heredity, it also calls attention to the shifting claims of retrogression theory, social "science" which argued that free blacks would revert to primitive behavior without slavery's "civilizing" influence. Though retrogression theory attempted to reorder the power structure of a slaveless society, in arguing that "black blood" predisposed one to moral corruption, it only exacerbated *dis*order. The ultimate legacy of retrogression theory was greater cultural confusion. As Joel Williamson has argued, this confusion influenced Southern culture's attitude toward moral deportment as well: "By about 1900 it was possible in the South for one who was biologically pure white to become black by behavior. A white person could cross over to blackness. Blackness and whiteness became a matter not just of color or even blood, but of inner morality reflected by outward performance" (467). Such pervasive attitudinal confusion suggests that attempting to define race more clearly only highlighted the ambivalence of racial differences. It is precisely this ambivalence that *The Autobiography of an Ex-Colored Man* problematizes and that the Ex-Colored Man himself embodies.

Having been born shortly after the close of the Civil War, the protagonist experiences childhood during a time of dramatic cultural transition, which was especially pronounced for individuals of mixed race. Moving north to Connecticut hardly shields the boy and his mother from incipient Jim Crowism, as Vann Woodward's work makes clear: "One of the strangest things about the career of Jim Crow," he writes, "is that the system was born in the North and reached an advanced age before moving South in force" (17). For a biracial American like the Ex-Colored Man, personal freedom and civic identity were legally and socially manipulated with alarming virulence.[2] The mother's ambivalent answer to the fraught question, "Am I white or am I nigger?" reflects the ambivalence of her social world and her historical moment, where the transient social position of the mulatto was articulated in the public attitude toward amalgamation. These years were characterized by volumes of miscegenation jurisprudence, laws passed that sought to determine race, to define one's racial status, to allow for or to prevent intermarriage. Volumes of legal history testify that defining, let alone denying, one's racial identity, was a complex and engrossing task.

The "am I white or am I nigger" scene is one of the book's most troubling moments: its echo resounds throughout the text. The narrator was born into a world in which a mulatto child was increasingly considered not to be a member of the "inferior" Negro race but actually beneath it. Had he been born into slavery, he would have clearly been considered black because his blackness would have served an economic purpose. As a black, he was property; he could increase his master's (presumably, his father's) capital. During slavery, the Ex-Colored Man would have received the best possible treatment afforded slaves because of his light skin. But following emancipation, the social position of mulattoes was given much more and quite different attention. In light of the biological and genetic theories that dominated discussions of race throughout the nineteenth century, mulattoes had to be publicly reinterpreted, lest the preferential treatment they were given as slaves make them demanding. This "science" served the ruling class because it established the mulatto's "mutant" status. As George M. Frederickson observes, "In 1857 J. Aitken Meigs . . . gave a scientist's view of the danger to the nation that would result from the fusing of diverse races. 'As long as the blood of one citizen . . . differs from that of another,' he asserted, 'diverse and probably long forgotten forms would crop out . . . as indications of the past, and obstacles to the assumption of that perfectly homogeneous character which be-

---

2. The mulatto figure is most dramatically vilified in Thomas Dixon's immensely popular 1903 novel *The Leopard's Spots*. Here, the nation itself is determined by racial purity: "*The future of the world depends on the future of this Republic. This Republic can have no future if racial lines are broken and its proud citizenship sinks to the level of a mongrel breed of Mulattoes*" (200).

longs to pure stocks alone'" (132). Even respected citizens and intellectuals who had no interest in supporting the Southern radicals who promoted this ideology, committed as it was to the social and political suffocation of blacks, were drawn in.

To consider these scientific theories about race in light of *The Autobiography of an Ex-Colored Man* is to recognize how fully James Weldon Johnson problematized his protagonist. Consider the following disturbing passage. In Georgia 1869, the very place and the very time of the narrator's birth, *State v. Scott* articulated the legal and social context into which he was born:

> The amalgamation of the races is not only unnatural, but is always productive of deplorable results. Our daily observation shows us, that the offending offspring of these unnatural connections are generally sickly and effeminate, and that they are inferior in physical development and strength to the full blood of either race. It is sometimes urged that such marriages should be encouraged, for the purpose of elevating the inferior race. The reply is, that such connections never elevate the inferior race to the position of the superior, but they bring down the superior to that of the inferior. They are productive of evil, and evil only, without any corresponding good. (qtd. Saks 64)

What is most difficult about reading this passage in light of *The Autobiography* is recognizing that many of the characteristics that the legal brief ascribes to mixed-race offspring are the very characteristics we find most prominent and annoying in the Ex-Colored Man. His story is riddled with accounts of his frailty and trepidation: as a child, he can barely withstand the trauma of a bath and recoils in fear from a fenced-in cow; as an adult, he shrinks from meeting the president of the University of Atlanta; his mother, "by her caresses and often her tears" often "encouraged" him into "fits of sentimental hysteria" (18). Weak, effeminate, far less physically defined than Red Head in his bulk, or Shiny in his striking presence, the narrator fulfills this negative stereotype of the mulatto with disturbing accuracy.

The mulatto's place in American society has never been fixed or certain; passing is but a tangible illustration of this legal and social fluctuation. Because the narrator's life spans a period in which the mulatto was increasingly viewed with social contempt, his passing parallels a national struggle to reconcile the antebellum belief in a "third category"—a not quite black and yet not fully white person—with the Plessy decision that rendered this third category legally impossible but, paradoxically, still physically viable. When the taxonomy of a third category is eliminated and yet the members of that category continue to exist, these members' presence continually calls attention to what Marjorie Garber refers to as "the impossibility of taxonomy, the fatal limitation of classification *as* segregation, the inevitability of miscegenation as misnomer" (274). Visibly white and yet socially cast as black, the narrator is forever displaced.

Like its protagonist, the narrative itself seems generically problematic. Numerous connections between James Weldon Johnson's genuine autobiography, *Along This Way* (1933), and his novel *The Autobiography of an Ex-Colored Man* invite us, for instance, to question how fictional the fiction really is. The differences between Johnson and the Ex-Colored Man have been usefully examined in two important studies that read *Along This Way* in relation to *The Autobiography of an Ex-Colored Man*. Many circumstances precluded James Weldon Johnson from passing for white: he was both too dark-skinned and too prominent as a civil rights leader, as a musician, and as a diplomat. Joseph T. Skerrett Jr.'s insightful analysis argues that in the novel, "Johnson symbolically objectified problems" from his own life and thereby "exorcised the weakness" that he saw in himself and in his friend D., a light-skinned colleague who did, in fact, pass for white. In this projection, Skerrett argues, the Ex-Colored Man comes to stand for "the temptation to desire and to seek a less heroic, less painful identity than their blackness imposed on them" (558). Valerie Smith also considers *Along This Way* in relation to *The Autobiography of an Ex-Colored Man*, and, like Skerrett, anchors her argument to the differences between the two texts: "These significant dissimilarities militate against our assuming Johnson's identity with his narrator and prompt us instead to maintain an ironic attitude toward the Ex-Colored Man" (46). Such analyses of the dissonance between the two autobiographies inevitably reinforce James Weldon Johnson's historical centrality as a black leader, as they foreground Johnson's own monumental contributions to civil rights and to African American culture generally.

Skerrett and Smith both rely on a principle of textual difference in order to analyze a text whose central premise itself challenges racial difference. By focusing on the dissonance between *Along This Way* and *The Autobiography of an Ex-Colored Man*, both critics refrain from fully considering the striking similarities of these two works: indeed, the Ex-Colored Man's similarity to white people creates much of the tension in

The Autobiography of an Ex-Colored Man. The whiteness of his skin constitutes a crisis of similarity as compelling as the crisis of difference constituted by the "blackness" of his blood. The similarities between the two texts make clear that Johnson was a crafty and innovative writer: coyly poking at the boundaries between fact and fiction, autobiography and novel, history and wish fulfillment, he also repudiates boundary itself—including, necessarily, that which separates black from white. Though *The Autobiography* was accepted by its intended audience as autobiography, that Johnson was in fact writing fiction-as-autobiography underscores the degree to which literary self-identity is consciously constructed.

To look at the similarities between the two texts, however, underscores Johnson's participation in American literary culture at large: as Werner Sollors has noted, *The Autobiography of an Ex-Colored Man* is "strikingly similar in literary strategy" to Abraham Cahan's 1913 "Autobiography of an American Jew" (*Beyond* 168). Moreover, it is a fact well worth noting that Johnson was not alone in misrepresenting the category of his literary composition as an autobiography.[3] For instance, Gertrude Stein's *The Autobiography of Alice B. Toklas,* a work that also manipulates genre in order to problematize the autonomy of her narrative persona, appeared in print in the same year as *Along This Way.* Literary self-generation has long been a hallmark of American identity; by situating *The Autobiography of an Ex-Colored Man* in this canon, we invite a more nuanced and complicated reading.

Striking repetitions, evident both in linguistic mimicry and in shared attitudes, challenge Johnson's claim that he composed *Along This Way* in part to explain that he was not, in fact, the Ex-Colored Man. Events in childhood resonated for both men: for Johnson, "spankings were literally dark moments in my life" (14); and the Ex-Colored Man also recalls "a terrific spanking . . . indelibly fixed . . . in my mind" (2). Johnson's

---

3. Johnson's refusal to claim authorship of the novel at its 1912 printing added to its literary intrigue. He was well aware of the risks he took in seeking anonymous publication: "as you know," he wrote to his friend George A. Towns, "critics are especially wary of anonymous stories purporting to be true" (Jackson 189). In *Along This Way,* Johnson hints at the delight he took in anonymity, when the "authorship of the book excited the curiosity of the literate colored people, and there was speculation among them as to who the writer might be" (238). In one instance, he listened in on a conversation where another man claimed to have written the book.

mother was his "first music teacher" and would play to him on the piano (14). As for the Ex-Colored Man, the "evenings on which [his mother] opened the little piano were the happiest hours of [his] childhood" (5). Both were voracious readers and would lay out on their parlor floors, gobbling up books. The romance of reading infected them both and influenced their attitudes. Johnson's childhood sweetheart was thus called "My Heart's Desire" (64); the Ex-Colored Man's, "she of the brown eyes" (25). This rhetorical similarity bears out other shared situations: both were composers of music and of texts, both traveled widely, both loved France. Johnson was greatly influenced by a wealthy, Byronic mentor, Dr. Thomas Osmond Summers, on whom the Ex-Colored Man's patron seems clearly modeled. When he arrived at Atlanta University, James Weldon Johnson noticed the girls: "They ranged in color from ebony black to milk white. At one end of the scale eyes were dark and hair crisp, and at the other eyes were blue or gray and the hair light and like fine spun silk" (75). The Ex-Colored Man sees this as well: "The colors ranged from jet black to pure white, with light hair and eyes. . . . And, too, I could not help noticing that many of the girls, particularly those of the delicate brown shades, with black eyes and wavy hair, were decidedly pretty" (44). Linguistic repetition and character sketches mimic ideological similarity: James Weldon Johnson, like the Ex-Colored Man, experiences adulthood as a time of coming to terms with his race, his bearing in his country. The two men saw the world in similar ways and expressed their visions in similar words.

Indeed, in the similarities between the two texts, we witness a resounding denunciation of racial categorization in America. In the two similar passages about Atlanta University, the range of colors illustrates the instability of racial boundaries. The presence of white skin at a black university captures the attention of both James Weldon Johnson and the Ex-Colored Man, and for good reason. The variety of shades and skin colors in evidence at Atlanta testify to the sheer inapplicability of clear black-and-white racial distinctions. Visible evidence misrepresents invisible ideology: the spectrum of skin tones Johnson twice describes illustrates the artificiality of any designated color line and, in so doing, reflects back on Albion Tourgée's argument for Homer Plessy. As Eric Sundquist astutely notes, by identifying whiteness as property, Tourgée invoked "an element of color that would destroy Jim Crow by rendering it chaotic" (247). The chaos of color described as a brilliant spectrum in both *The Autobiography of an Ex-Colored Man* and *Along This Way* rhetorically illustrates the fundamental impracticality of *Plessy v. Ferguson*.

"Perhaps more than any other literary form in black American letters," William L. Andrews writes, "autobiography has been recognized and celebrated since its inception as a powerful means of addressing and altering sociopolitical as well as cultural realities in the United States" (Introduction 1). Surely, the democratic nature of autobiography as a genre has been well established in relation to the American canon at large. Albert E. Stone believes that autobiography is a profoundly comprehensive form: "it is simultaneously historical record and literary confession, didactic essay and ideological testament" (2). And William Dean Howells writes that it is "the most democratic province in the republic of letters" ("Autobiography" 798). But we do well to heed Andrews's warning about "the wisdom of evaluating black American autobiographies according to standard assumptions about how life, self, and writing interact in the tradition of Western autobiography" (Introduction 3). In *The Autobiography of an Ex-Colored Man,* Johnson is self-conscious about the mythical status of success-story autobiographies and responds through a parody of the formulaic "rags to riches" trope. In particular, themes and scenes that evoke Booker T. Washington's *Up from Slavery* and Benjamin Franklin's autobiography provide Johnson with an opportunity to critique the ideological construction of these handbooks to a segregated American identity.

If the autobiographies of Franklin and Washington represent lives rendered idealistic through each author's fictional embellishment, the Ex-Colored Man's autobiography represents a fictional life rendered quotidian through the hypothetical author's essential ambivalence. All three autobiographies share fundamental concerns—questioning social mobility, rejecting generational relations, emphasizing the individual. Yet the Ex-Colored Man's self-contradictory account of his life boldly reveals what Franklin and Washington struggle to conceal: the significant gaps between representation and reality, between earned accomplishments and serendipity, between one's masks and one's true self. Laura Browder's excellent analysis of ethnic impersonator autobiographies is worth considering here, for like *The Autobiography of an Ex-Colored Man,* these impersonators call attention to the paradox created when, "by playing into cultural stereotypes of their newly chosen ethnicities, they have mired their readers further in essentialist thinking" (2). The mythical handbooks to self-generation and success for both white and black American are thus exposed and collapsed. "While ethnic impersonators may free themselves from the historical trap of an unwanted identity by passing into a new one," Browder explains, "their success rests on their ability to manipulate stereotypes, thus further miring their audience in essentialist racial and ethnic categories" (10).

Through pointed analogies, Johnson insists that neither Franklin's nor Washington's autobiographical account accurately depicts his experience. When, at the end of the book, The Ex-Colored Man is resigned to living as a white man, Johnson's narrator becomes enmeshed in the sort of class struggle and work ethic through which Benjamin Franklin framed national values generations earlier. The "newly white" narrator parodies Franklin's life and rise to success. Like Franklin, he grows industrious, humbly asserting, "I did my work faithfully, and received a rise of salary before I expected it" (142). Once his financial stability is assured, the narrator becomes increasingly attracted to the mechanization of the marketplace. Heeding Benjamin Franklin's calls to thrift and modesty, he reaps Franklin's promised rewards—wealth: "What an interesting and absorbing game is money-making! After each deposit at my savings bank I used to sit and figure out, all over again, my principal and interest, and make calculations on what the increase would be in such and such a time. Out of this I derived great pleasure. I denied myself as much as possible in order to swell my savings" (142). Independence, thrift, deferring of rewards, hard work: the goals that now motivate the Ex-Colored Man are fueled by his lust for wealth. And this is a particular brand of wealth, for it is not the opulence of his benefactor, whose sole objective was pleasure and luxury; rather, he demonstrates a commitment to capitalism. The narrator accumulates wealth in the spirit of a true financier: a Protestant work-ethic American, he designs his life with repression and self-interest, filtering his funds through a particular national ideology. Yet in spite of his white life fulfilling all the promises of an idealized white America, it is empty. The narrator feels, in spite of his success, "small and selfish" (154). A moral and spiritual vacuum apparently accompanies the Ex-Colored Man's financial success.

The Autobiography of an Ex-Colored Man challenges the myths of black American success as well. If Benjamin Franklin's ideology is rendered suspect for its hollowness, the historic black ideologies are similarly debunked. Johnson consciously rejects the conciliatory disposition of

Booker T. Washington, thus refusing to be restricted by the narrowness of Washington's apparent self-abnegation. This is most clear in the narrator's decision not to attend Atlanta University. The Ex-Colored Man's hesitation, his inability to pursue an education, his reluctance to ask for help—all these characteristics offer a dramatic departure from the model of energy and industriousness provided in Booker T. Washington's *Up from Slavery*. Washington's resolution is the stuff that myths are made of: "I was on fire constantly with one ambition," he writes, "and that was to go to Hampton" (30). To reach Hampton, Washington suffers humiliation, sleeps under city sidewalks, unloads cargoes of pig iron to earn money for food, begs rides, and walks a good portion of the five hundred mile journey. "A factual view of slavery, for Washington," Andrews notes, "is concerned less with a static concept of historical truth, frozen in the past, than with the need for rhetorical power in the ever-evolving present" ("Representation" 83). Washington takes pride in proving himself worthy of matriculation and exploits every opportunity Hampton provides.

Standing alongside this model of achievement on the shelves of American literature, the Ex-Colored Man's narrative appears a countertext, the antimyth. Homeless and orphaned, he carelessly allows himself to be robbed of the money that would have paid for his education, spinelessly refuses to confront the likely thief, and then awkwardly decides to abandon his opportunity. What distinguishes the Ex-Colored Man's unsuccessful pursuit of an education from Booker T. Washington's successful one is his reluctance to ask for help from social and intellectual superiors. The prospect of any outward show of self-effacement paralyzes him: "As I neared the grounds, the thought came across me, would not the story sound fishy? Would it not place me in the position of an imposter or beggar? What right had I to worry these busy people with the results of my carelessness? If the money could not be recovered, which I doubted that it could, what good would it do to tell them about it? The shame and embarrassment which the whole situation gave me caused me to stop at the gate. I paused, undecided for a moment; then turned and slowly retraced my steps, and so changed the whole course of my life" (45). One way to reconsider his reluctance to explain his misfortune and ask for help is to recognize that the narrator refuses what Booker T. Washington had previously embraced: a model of apprenticeship and obligation that reinforces patriarchal rule. Having been rejected by his father, the narrator in turn rejects patriarchal models—both their demands and their rewards. And while he feels no compunction in accepting a loan from the railroad porter, to ingratiate himself to the president of Atlanta University would be to participate in a hierarchical model of society rather than a democratic community sustained by peers.[4] But a more provocative and instructive interpretation would read the Ex-Colored Man's insistent critique of American race relations in terms of both his white and his black literary forbears. Johnson's text is then not simply or solely a celebration of the sort of individualism presented by Benjamin Franklin, it also is a damning critique of it. It is not only a longing for the kind of community and "work so glorious" that he laments at the end but also an ironic evaluation of the price of such community, such work.

Johnson's work, both in *The Autobiography* and in his life's writing, seeks persistently to resolve the challenge posed by another influential literary forebear, Hector St. John de Crevecoeur when he asked, "What then is this new man, the American?" Johnson is no less concerned with the fundamental philosophical dilemma of national identity than were authors who are considered canonical or mainstream. Passing offers the Ex-Colored Man access to a particularly American form of success: financial security, social prominence, personal independence. But *The Autobiography of an Ex-Colored Man* is also a book about all sorts of passing: about mobility that is social and physical as well as racial. It demonstrates, ultimately, that there are no essences in a world that offers social mobility; one is, legitimately, what one makes of one's self. By avoiding this central theme, we have for years ignored the novel's rich implications: the Ex-Colored Man is prototypically an American literary character, one who seeks a success that transcends class-bound hierarchies, that is defined by merit rather than race, and that allows one to offer a better life to one's children than was available to one's parents. In fact, through his racial vacillation, the Ex-Colored Man locates his self-invention in an identity that is both sympathetic to many races and independent of any single racial affiliation.

---

4. This point is reinforced when the Ex-Colored Man repays the fifteen-dollar loan: he borrows it from another friend, perhaps one of those whom he has often treated to drinks (61).

4 | Passing and the "Fast Yellowing Manuscripts"

WHEN JEAN TOOMER'S *Cane* was published in 1923, David Levering Lewis reports, "Harlem and Afro-America welcomed what promised to be a major contender for the Great American Novel" (59). Hardly hyperbolic, Lewis's assessment characterizes the understanding among cultural analysts, literary critics, and historians that Jean Toomer inspired writers who would produce the literature of the Harlem Renaissance and, indeed, the twentieth century's black canon. The stylistic innovations in *Cane* expanded the possibilities of literary modernism (as he wrote it, Toomer corresponded often with his friend and mentor Waldo Frank, then part of white New York's literary vanguard) and its poignant evocations of black life, North and South, articulated a world never before rendered with such eloquence. Yet just as the structure of *Cane* moves according to a cycle between South and North, prose and poetry, rural and urban (fragments of semicircles separate each section so as to underscore the point), Jean Toomer's life was organized around his vacillation between black and white (numerous autobiographical manuscripts articulate this so as to underscore the point). Toomer's insistence on racial self-determination is nowhere more clear than in his audacious assertion in a letter to Horace Liveright, "My racial composition and my position in the world are realities which I alone may determine" (5 Sept. 1923). Though Toomer continually characterized his racial individualism as being wholly American (for instance, naming himself "the first American" on the basis of his racial hybridity), the Supreme Court's ruling in *Plessy v. Ferguson* was handed down less than two years after he was born. The Supreme Court, as he well knew, made a very different determination.

Like James Weldon Johnson's Ex-Colored Man, who guards a box of treasured documents, "fast yellowing manuscripts" that symbolize for him "the only tangible remnants of a vanished dream, a dead ambition, a sacrificed talent" (154), Jean Toomer also guarded a box of "precious, private possessions" throughout his life. His box, however, contained not the "yellowing" evidence of a renounced black racial identity, but rather the letter in which his great aunt Adeline B. Saffold encouraged his grandfather to do as she did—to pass for white. As Robert B. Jones reports, the 1863 letter remained in the Pinchback family for years and "became the property of Jean Toomer, who preserved it as a family heirloom" (5). Indeed, Toomer's widow retained possession of the letter even after his death, and Jones quotes from it at length. Its impassioned tone—addressed, ironically enough, to "Pink," a nickname that also colloquially refers to a white person—conveys a sister's concern for her brother's survival as much as for his financial or personal success: "If I were you Pink I would not let my ambition die. I would seek to rise and not in that class either but I would take my position in the world as a white man as you are and let the other go for be assured of this as the other you will *never* get your rights. Know this that the *mobs* are constantly breaking out in different parts of the north and even in Canada against the oppressed colored race. Right in Cincinnati they can hardly walk the streets but they are attacked. . . . *I* have nothing to do with the Negroes am *not* one of them. Take my advise *dear* brother and do the same" (qtd. in Jones 5). Adeline Saffold frames her advice with images of mob violence, precisely the "sense of alarm" (134) that arouses the Ex-Colored Man from his bed prior to his firsthand witnessing of a lynching. The Ex-Colored Man was able to watch the horror unfold only because his "identity as a colored man had not yet become known in the town" (135), so he took his position in the crowd as a white man. In its argumentative strategy and its rhetorical crafting, Adeline Saffold's letter urging her brother to pass for white evokes the moment in which Johnson's Ex-Colored Man decides to pass for white. "I argued that to forsake one's race to better one's condition was no less worthy an action," the Ex-Colored Man explains, "than to forsake one's country for the same purpose" (139). Shunning identification with what Adeline Saffold terms "the oppressed colored race," the Ex-Colored Man decides "that it was not necessary for [him] to go about with a label of inferiority pasted across [his] forehead" (139).

The importance of this letter is evident in the care Toomer took to preserve it throughout his life,[1] and its symbolic resonance has much to offer in relation to Toomer's own supposed passing. But the letter's urgings—

---

1. Kerman and Eldridge report that "The box where this letter was kept was available only to Jean Toomer during his lifetime" (19 fn 7).

its insistence on the right of an individual to self-determination—also appear to have influenced Toomer's autobiographical and critical writings. For instance, in a cultural critique he wrote in 1929 for the French journal *Cahiers de l'Etoile* as part of a forum seeking to survey the American scene, Toomer's essay reveals not only his concern for the integrity and importance of the individual, but also his understanding of the broader implications of individual behavior. In "Opinions on the Questions of the *Cahiers de l'Etoile*," as he notes that unrest aids creativity by unsettling assumptions and expectations, he writes, "In time of panic a person does well to save himself. And yet, the difficulty is, that there is no saving of an individual: more than one must go up, or all will go down." Later, a 1934 essay about Alfred Steiglitz again takes up the topic, when he honors Steiglitz as "An *individual* who is himself, who is for those of the wide world that claim him by similarity of spirit and of values" ("The Hill" 98). Toomer's cultural criticism thus demonstrates his ongoing efforts to mediate the divisive legacy so richly illustrated here, in the familial conflict between his great aunt's letter urging individual survival and his grandfather's political career promoting black civil rights.[2]

Their similar embrace of important, racially coded (that is, "fast yellowing") documents is not all that connects Toomer to the Ex-Colored Man, either symbolically or actually. One could parallel Toomer's penchant to misspell *Cane* as "Cain" to the Ex-Colored Man's own Biblical evocation of Jacob and Esau when he concludes, "I cannot repress the thought that, after all, I have chosen the lesser part, that I have sold my birthright for a mess of pottage" (154). Charles Scruggs argues that the biblical Cain and his descendants haunt Toomer's *Cane* and provide

---

2. Toomer's maternal grandfather, P. B. S. Pinchback, the powerful Reconstruction politician, openly declared his African descent, Pinchback's mother having been Eliza Benton Stewart, the multiracial former slave and mistress of the wealthy white planter Major William Pinchback. Lerone Bennett Jr. cites Pinchback's speech before a skeptical Senate on first arriving in Washington, wherein one can see his evocation of the community. "'Sir,' he told the Senate, 'I demand simple justice. I am here not as a beggar. I do not care so far as I am personally concerned whether you give me my seat or not. I will go back to my people and come here again; but I will tell you to preserve your own consistency. Do not make fish of me while you make flesh of everybody else'" (243–44). Pinchback's political skill and his personal charm are in evidence here, and one can see why W. E. B. Du Bois would characterize him as "a practical politician [who] played the politician's game" (*Black Reconstruction* 469). Alice Walker, however, regards Pinchback as "a racial opportunist" who "did nothing of substance for the masses of black men who voted for him" (63).

clues to the work's spiritual design. The nomadic Cain, whose cursed mark "can be interpreted as a badge of protection as well as of shame," comes to symbolize, for Toomer, "the African in a hostile land," a figure evocative of the Great Migration (278). In this way, Scruggs suggests, Toomer's work evokes larger American literary themes that have always "tended to mythologize experience" (290). He insists, therefore, that "it is not by accident that Toomer wanted to depict the black experience in mythic terms" (277). Certainly, the Ex-Colored Man's final questioning lament likewise invites his readers to read his tale's broadest meanings.

One also notes the rootlessness shared by both: the five years following Toomer's high school graduation recall the aimless wanderings of the Ex-Colored Man. Orphaned, ambivalently racialized, torn between duty to the self and duty to their family's values, both men sought an elusive something. In "Outline of the Story of the Autobiography" (20:514), an undated typescript, Jean Toomer recounts his own youthful wanderlust, noting "I literally batted about America" (21). Literally batted indeed: Toomer undertook and then abandoned the study of agriculture in Madison, Wisconsin; he attended the Massachusetts College of Agriculture in Amherst; he lived in New York until he ran out of money; he headed for Chicago, to the American College of Physical Training; he spent that summer at Wheaton College and in the fall, enrolled for classes at the University of Chicago at Midway. He studied sociology at the City College of New York, then history; he went to Washington, D.C., to register for the war but was rejected. He returned to Chicago, lived at a fraternity house, and sold Fords. He relocated to Milwaukee to accept a substitute's job as a physical education director. He returned to Washington, D.C., where his grandfather's disappointment in him made him miserable. He returned to New York, to a sales position, and took up piano. He had a breakdown; he vacillated between Washington and New York, bumming his way back and forth. In the summer of 1920, he returned, yet again, to Washington, D.C., to write.

Toomer's geographical wandering during the years before he devoted himself to writing are also reflected in the generic permutations of *Cane,* as Werner Sollors has made clear. "Toomer's *Cane* (1923), a book that significantly defies genre categorization, is an experimental search for reality beyond labels and for mankind above race and nationality," he writes. "Toomer expressed a complex vision of the new America of the future. He wanted his readers to understand the essential unity beyond phenomenal diversity, including that created by ethnic categories" (*Beyond Ethnicity* 253). Toomer's desire to articulate an individual voice—free of what he saw as the restrictive, artificially narrow confines of segregation's logic—thus manifested itself in experimental forms in *Cane*. Yet *Cane* represents but a fraction of the writing that Toomer produced, and the fact that he is best remembered for *Cane* alone testifies to the intractability of the very categories he most fervently sought to elide.

Jean Toomer's "fast yellowing manuscripts" collected over the years, as he wrote cultural and literary criticism, spiritual treatises, poetry, and autobiographies that failed, time and time again, to find a publisher. If the Ex-Colored Man's unseen documents represent "a vanished dream, a dead ambition, a sacrificed talent," Jean Toomer's long unpublished works reflect the impossibility of finding an audience receptive to his vision of race and, indeed, his definition of America. One might well chart the history of both African American literary criticism and what George Hutchinson so accurately terms "American racial discourse" by mapping Jean Toomer's career—its successes and failures, both in Toomer's lifetime and since his death ("Discourse" 226). The availability of Toomer's work now, its acceptance or rejection by publishers, and its current and past critical and popular reception are all factors indicative of his shifting status. But this shifting status is more importantly, if also more elusively, evidence of the shift in the critical approach to passing. Just as *Cane* owes its "recovery" to the emergence of African American studies programs, a direct result of both the Black Arts and Black Power movements of the late 1960s, so too does his current popularity among critics emerge from the heightened attention to racial indeterminacy, the so-called social construction of race and essentialism.

The first issue of *Cane* in 1923 was a critical success, but it never achieved popular acclaim; indeed, Charles Scruggs declares it "an instant failure" ("Mark of Cain" 277). Though a limited reprint in 1927 (the same year as the successful reissue of *The Autobiography of an Ex-Colored Man*) attempted to capitalize on the widespread appeal of Harlem writers, Toomer's work never attracted the audience that Johnson's did. The next hardcover reprint appeared in 1969, when, as Henry Louis Gates Jr.'s survey of the critical history of African American studies makes clear, "the field . . . benefitted from a great outburst of interest" ("African" 304). Though this energy focused on art, its motivation was political, as "the black arts movement of the mid-1960's has declared literature, and especially poetry, to be the cultural wing of the black power revolution" (304–05), and critical engagement with *Cane* at this time reflected these goals. *Cane* offered a rich celebration of folk culture, and the seminal critics who helped establish, authorize, and legitimize black studies took note. To give but one representative example, Bernard Bell celebrates how Toomer "uses [folk] songs as symbols of the spiritual resiliency of rural black Americans and, by extension, of the souls of a new order of man" (98). Many studies of this time reflect the importance of *Cane* to scholars working to transform the literary critical establishment. Gates explains their agenda: "they shared a concern with the literariness of African American works, as they wrestled to make these texts a proper object of analysis within traditional departments of English. . . . If the 'blackness' of a text was to be found anywhere, they argued, it would be in the practical uses of language" ("African" 305). The extraordinary lyricism of *Cane* thus offered much: critics extolled the genius of Toomer's use of blues, call and response, the veil, authenticity, double-consciousness—all the tropes of Afrocentric literary study.[3]

Still, though the 1969 reissue of *Cane* received considerable critical attention, Toomer's voluminous collection of autobiographical sketches, philosophical treatises, spiritual tracts, cultural criticism, and racial statements languished in near obscurity. When these works were excerpted for reissue in Darwin T. Turner's important 1980 collection, *The Wayward and the Seeking,* the volume was used by scholars as a far more authoritative statement than, in fact, it is. *The Wayward and the Seeking* included a mere smattering of Toomer's autobiographical work, and these excerpts were heavily edited. Its impact is best articulated by Charles Scruggs and Lee VanDemarr: "Turner himself was clear in his introduction about the selective nature of the autobiographical fragments he joined together to produce a narrative of Toomer's life through 1923. But inevitably the largest portion of the autobiographical writings were excluded from this anthology, and some of those excluded pages are of crucial significance for understanding Toomer's po-

---

3. See, for instance, Houston Baker, "Journey toward Black Art: Jean Toomer's *Cane,*" *Singers at Daybreak* (Washington: Howard UP, 1974); Barbara Bowen, "Untroubled Voice: Call-and-Response in *Cane,*" *Black American Literature Forum* 16 (1982): 12–18; Charles T. Davis, "Jean Toomer and the South: Region and Race within a Literary Imagination," *Studies in the Literary Imagination* 28 (1975) 423–34; Clifford Mason, "Jean Toomer's Black Authenticity." *Black World* 20.1 (1970): 70–76.

litical life" (5–6). Both within academe and without, the narrative of Toomer's life that emerges from Turner's introduction has become the default biography. Alice Walker's review of the Turner collection, which first appeared in the *New York Times* and then was included in her important volume *In Search of Our Mother's Gardens,* authorizes the collection as one that "does much to clarify the Jean Toomer mystery" (61), primarily by revealing what Walker reads as Toomer's racial opportunism combined with his willful blindness to racism. Counterposing these autobiographical writings against *Cane,* she laments his decision to "live his own life as a white man. . . . because it appears this choice undermined Toomer's moral judgement" (62). Walker's review sounded a note that would echo throughout much subsequent criticism of Toomer and of *Cane,* a note in which his self-identification is understood to have broader moral implications.

The difference between Toomer's public (published) expressions of racial identity and those that remain unpublished—either because they were never intended for publication, such as letters or daybook entries, or because they never found a receptive audience, such as his autobiographies and racial tracts—is one that both reflects and shapes American racial discourse, public and private. Because passing, as Pamela Caughie so shrewdly observes, is "one of the practices through which we try to refuse the identities that have been historically offered to us and that continue to structure our responses even or especially when we seek to move out of them" (5), the publication or publishability of one or another identity is determined by forces beyond an individual's control. In the case of Jean Toomer, this lack of control clearly evinces itself and illustrates the truth of Michael T. Gilmore's observation that "politics can effect these conflicting results within the career of one single author, stirring him or her to bursts of productivity and then stunting the very talent it has liberated, driving the writer to silence or to the protracted suicide of drink and despair" ("Two Cases" 199). The same might be said of an author's critical legacy; the recent issue of additional collections of Jean Toomer's previously unavailable work reflects the critical engagement with a more complicated sense of race and racial difference.

To give an example, in "The Crock of Problems," written in 1928 but unpublished until 1996, Toomer poses the question "To what race do I belong?" His answer repudiates even the premise of passing because it rejects the rules of color division through which passing is constituted. "It is evident at once," Toomer writes, "that none of the standard color labels can do anything but misrepresent me. They do not fit" (56). But he holds his own history up—specifically, strikingly—against James Weldon Johnson's fiction. "The factors which cause a person to wish to 'pass' for white," he notes, "are well described in James Weldon Johnson's *The Autobiography of an Ex-Colored Man*" (57). Even as he raises the parallel, Toomer simultaneously distances himself from such an association. When writing about his own experience of what others would term to be passing, Toomer insists that it was not passing: "In my own experience among the racial groups I have not had the psychological state which obtains when one passes or tries to pass. I have never tried to pass simply because I have never had to try. I have simply gone and lived here and there. I have been what I am. Sometimes I saw fit to say that I had Negro blood. Sometimes I did not" (58). When Toomer describes how he has crossed the color line with ease and without compromising his sense of personal identity, he fully expects that his self-assurance confounds both sides of the color line. He both acknowledges and distances himself from whites who want to believe that racial mimicry is easily detectable as well as from blacks who presume that adopting whiteness fosters a sense of betrayal and constant self-doubt. In this essay as elsewhere, Toomer defies the racialist ideology of his time and ours by refusing to accept prevailing standards for race consciousness.

By refusing to identify his own passing as passing, Toomer deliberately refuses to accept what he considers an arbitrarily designated racial identity. "I have simply gone and lived here and there," Toomer declares, employing the Ex-Colored Man's reasoning exactly. "I finally made up my mind that I would neither disclaim the black race nor claim the white race," the Ex-Colored Man asserts as he explains his decision to pass, "but that I would change my name, raise a mustache, and let the world take me for what it would" (139). More adamant than the Ex-Colored Man, who acknowledges at the book's end, "I am an ordinarily successful white man" (154), Toomer not only denies that he is passing, he also denies that passing has anything to do with racial categorization. His sense of self-identity substitutes a nationalist sense of self for a racialist one; and he proposes that all Americans rise above racialist ways of thinking in order to bypass race itself. "I am at once no one of the races and I am all of them," he writes. "I belong to no one of them and I belong to all. I am, in a strict racial sense, a member of a new race. . . . In so far as race and nationality are concerned, I wish to be known as an American" (58–59). Thus Jean Toomer attempted publicly to engage the conflicts associated with racial authenticity, racial authority, and authorship, yet he found limited success in publishing such engagements. In public as in private, Toomer faced hostility and adversity regarding his racial makeup; clearly, the legal and social conventions of his time defined him as black. "But to try to tie me to one of my parts," he wrote to Waldo Frank, "is surely to loose [sic] me" (Dec. 1922).

The absence of this perspective from much scholarship on Jean Toomer—not only a failure to reference Toomer's numerous unpublished essays and their political content, but also to acknowledge Waldo Frank's singular influence and to present fully Toomer's engagement with civil rights, socialism, and African American politics—has been elided through the ontological slipperiness of passing itself. Toomer's autobiographical writings pose special problems, for as William L. Andrews reminds us, "Autobiography holds a position of priority, indeed many would say preeminence, among the narrative traditions of black America" (Introduction 1). Often self-contradicting, repetitive, inaccurate, and evasive, Toomer's voluminous unpublished autobiographical writings testify to the self-serving machinations within his published autobiographical writings and reveal the slipperiness of the form in his hands.

Yet, as Andrews observes, it is precisely because autobiography "has played a leading role in the deconstruction of myths that assume a universal Western standard by which all autobiographies could be measured" (Introduction 3) that black American autobiographies in general and Jean Toomer's written account of himself in particular demand special consideration. The lack of gender specificity of the name *Jean* corresponds to the lack of racial specificity that virtually defined him, personally and artistically. Indeed, his own correspondence aptly illustrates a moment when the uncertainty of the two converge: Knopf publishers insistently addressed several letters to "Miss Jean Toomer"; and a letter from Claude A. Barnett of the Associated Negro Press begins, "For sometime we . . . have wondered who and also what you are."

Toomer himself also often wondered who and what he was. He not only had numerous childhood nicknames, but he changed his name legally and socially many times. In a brilliant essay titled "Jean Toomer and American Racial Discourse," George Hutchinson argues, "No doubt it is a fact of the first importance that Toomer was a self-named man"

(227). Toomer's biographers Cynthia Kerman and Richard Eldridge note that he "liked this individualization of names and absorbed from his grandfather the penchant for creating names to suit the person, occasion, and mood" (29). He finally settled on the name Jean Toomer when he began writing. These changes reflected an uncertainty about his familial identity: Toomer's father was absent from his life except in the son's imagination. Yet even in the family to which Toomer's relation was certain, racial stability was persistently unsettled. "In all of his self-definitions," Hutchinson writes, "Toomer dwells intensely on his racial identity, which he specifically differentiates from the races now acknowledged and named in the public discourse of the United States" ("Discourse" 227).

Toomer consistently and vehemently denounced racial categorization, and he argued for substituting a new nationalism—a new "America"—for the old racialism. Yet this premise has often been critically translated right back into a paradigm dependent on segregation logic. George Hutchinson notes that the critical penchant for designating Toomer as black "has curiously and ironically empowered his voice by fitting it anew within the very 'American' racial discourse whose authority he radically, incessantly disputed" ("Discourse" 227). Hutchinson demonstrates that the "difficulty of speaking or writing from outside the dominant discourse of race is a pervasive motif throughout *Cane*, and it has been matched by the difficulty of reading the text *against* the boundaries of that discourse" ("Discourse" 227). The trap remains the same: "a discourse that allows no room for a 'biracial' text (except by defining it as black) is part of the *same discursive system* that denies the identity of the person who defines himself or herself as both black and white (or, in Langston Hughes's phrase, 'neither white nor black'). Critics routinely ignore Toomer's idea that, as 'black' is to 'white' identity, the 'American' identity (in Toomer's sense) is to the 'black/white' identity" (228). Hutchinson's analysis demonstrates the intractability of binary opposition in our racial discourse. All roads lead back to segregation logic. The critical predisposition to read Toomer only through the very rubric he most vehemently rejected best illustrates the central paradox of America's racial ideology.

Toomer's racial self-identification has rarely been taken seriously by critics who insist on reading *Cane* primarily and strictly as a black text. Most agree with Alice Walker that "Toomer apparently used his 'connection' to black people only once, when it was to his advantage to do so" (64), and thereby endorse the view that *Cane* exploited racial identity. But Toomer understood the biracial or multiracial person to exist outside the black-white divide. Developing a sense of spiritual and intellectual selfhood became the central tenet of Toomer's adult life, a pursuit that took its strongest and most entangled hold on him after *Cane*. The unpublished typescript "'The Second River' or 'From Exile into Being'" describes a mystical experience in which Toomer felt himself born into a new and wholly fulfilled identity that was distinctly independent of corporeality. For a writer whose professional life was determined by his corporeal self—his body offering evidence of whiteness and blackness alternately—this subject is both racially charged and potentially subversive. "From Exile into Being" separates body from being. Here, bodies are sure and certain symbols of race: "What a fix the body is in. On the one hand, it is obstructed; on the other, it is spurred to act—by its captive. Inhibited, and yet driven; blocked *and* goaded; bound, yet told to move—not only by its captive, but also by other bodies and their prisoners. What a diabolical fix" (6).[4] This ostensible meditation on spiritual fulfillment also uncannily evokes the diabolical fix of a potential lynching, even as it articulates the sense of captivity Toomer feels about his own multiracial self.

Though Toomer himself explicitly repudiated the Ex-Colored Man as a model for passing, he explicitly claims another mentor and another text as his racial counterpart: Waldo Frank and his 1923 novel *Holiday*. There is much to link the two men and their works *Cane* and *Holiday*: most strikingly, they envisioned their works as counterparts, and they encouraged Boni and Liveright to publish and promote them in tandem. Indeed, as George Hutchinson notes, *Holiday* itself developed the theme

---

4. Janet Whyde has argued that for Toomer, "the body is a problematic sign of one's race, and some results of this problematic sign are fragmentation and division." Whyde believes that in *Cane,* "Toomer's goal is to reconcile and unify these opposites" (43), yet as Rudolph P. Byrd and especially Robert B. Jones have demonstrated, this impulse toward reconciliation also bore heavily on Toomer's autobiographical writing, and his spiritual and mystical work and writing—that is, on a much broader range of writing. See Rudolph P. Byrd, *Jean Toomer's Years with Gurdjieff* (Athens: U of Georgia P, 1990) for a fuller rendering of Toomer's "ideal of Man," which Byrd describes as "man as a psychologically and spiritually whole being" (xv) in relation to Gurdjieff (see note 7 below). Robert B. Jones, in *Jean Toomer and the Prison House of Thought*, examines Toomer's idealism as a reaction to his alienation; Jones's introduction to *Jean Toomer: Selected Essays and Literary Criticism* also surveys a fuller range of Toomer's prose.

that America "was destined to be the place where each race would give to the other what it lacked" (*Black and White* 108), and the history of the novel's origins, development, execution, revision, and publication all bear this out. Toomer and Frank's vision of their books as companion pieces grew out of their personal and intellectual intimacy, a relationship whose complexities and counterintuitive nuances have been neglected by many critics. Clearly, Toomer's friendship with Waldo Frank grew in part from his strong sense that Frank shared his vision of America, so it is wholly relevant and entirely consistent with Toomer's attitude toward American racial discourse that he would help Frank "pass" for "black" during a trip south and that he would deny that such passing even *was* passing.[5] Waldo Frank, for his part, believed that he shared Jean Toomer's sense of race and of passing, yet the accounts of their trip, their relationship, and their eventual estrangement tell a different story.

The image of the body as representative of racial authenticity, or of a racially authentic text, is one that informs Jean Toomer's relationship with Waldo Frank. "May I ask you, aside from giving me your general aesthetic impressions, to go into details with me?" Frank writes, as he sends Toomer part one of *Holiday*. He seeks corrections and suggestions "as to language, 'business', anything else that occurs to you. You know, the spirit of this world is nearer to me than its body. If you can help me, where I may have gone off as regards the body, I shall be indeed obliged."[6] Thus, Adeline B. Saffold's letter to P. B. S. Pinchback, so carefully preserved by Toomer throughout his life, is not the only epistle that offers insights into the writer's iconoclastic sense of race. He was similarly attentive to the preservation of his own correspondence, and the letters he wrote to Frank in particular—many carefully recorded with carbon paper and preserved throughout his life—underscore both the complexity and the heretofore undertheorized contradictions of his position. Waldo Frank was such an established writer that he seems to fit into a tradition of literary mentors—one thinks of William Dean Howells's sponsorship of Paul Laurence Dunbar, or of Carl Van Vechten and Langston Hughes, or of Fannie Hurst and Zora Neale

---

5. Though I am reluctant to overuse quotation marks as a way to problematize the terms I employ, it seems crucial to me to indicate that the idea of passing for black in this argument is more a construction of critics than a concept Toomer would have used.

6. Jean Toomer papers; though this letter is dated 16 January 1922 in Jean Toomer's pencil, the accuracy of the date seems questionable, as Frank didn't start writing *Holiday* until after the Spartanburg trip in the late summer of that year.

Hurston. In all of these relationships, white sponsors of black artists encourage and promote young talent but pay the historical price of being remembered primarily as patronizing, a legacy rendered all the more tortured because of the political implications of their racial difference.

Jean Toomer's autobiographical writings exacerbated this legacy by incorrectly charging that Frank betrayed him when he wrote an introduction to *Cane* that emphasized Toomer's black ancestry, rather than presenting the more nuanced, multiethnic identification that Toomer preferred. The autobiographical selections included in Darwin T. Turner's collection *The Wayward and the Seeking* underscore the point. There, Toomer explains his quandary over the preface: "my need to have the book published was so great, but my suspicions as to Waldo Frank's lack of understanding of, or failure to accept, my actuality became active again. . . . it was thus through Frank's agency that an erroneous picture of me was put in the minds of certain people in New York before my book came out. Thus was started a misunderstanding in the very world, namely the literary art world, in which I expected to be really understood" (126). Some scholars do note another reason for the split—that Toomer ran off with Frank's wife—but insofar as this account suggests the counterintuitive notion that Toomer betrayed Frank, it is often dismissed or, at best, noted briefly in passing. Critics who see Toomer only as a black man who tried to pass for white tend to simplify his history in order to render him a victim of racist thinking. Several factors contribute to the staying power of this latter impression. For one, Waldo Frank was a private man, and even his memoirs present "a quite scrupulous avoidance of details of private family affairs" (Trachtenberg viii). When he does mention Toomer in the memoirs, Frank's references make no mention of Toomer's role in his divorce. Instead, he compliments Toomer's "lush genius" and laments that "In his need to forget he was Negro, he joined the transcendental pseudo-Hindu cult of Gurdjieff" (107).[7] Onita Estes-Hicks offers an extreme—and particularly vitriolic—account of the break,

---

7. The psychological system developed by Georges Ivanovich Gurdjieff (1877–1949) sought to integrate spiritual and social reform through an intense investigation into human potential. Gurdjieff's system proposed alleviating humanity's essential incompleteness by studying what each individual might become, by encouraging the development of one's inner qualities. The system found its fullest expression in the Institute for the Harmonious Development of Man, which was housed at the Chateau Le Prieure de Fountainbleau-Avon, France, in October 1922.

arguing that Toomer, "new to the literary intrigue and malice of New York, became un-nerved by the behavior of Frank," but that he "continued to struggle valiantly" nevertheless (27). This interpretation seems clearly to embrace Toomer's version without question and without considering contemporaneous evidence (in particular, letters between Frank and Toomer) that suggests a different account.[8] By contrast, after a careful review of all evidence, Charles Scruggs and Lee VanDemarr present an excellent and compelling account of the two men's interactions. They conclude: "In explaining his attitude about race, Toomer's assessments of 'Waldo Frank's lack of understanding of, or failure to accept, my actuality' seems accurate. But in attempting to present his version of how that 'actuality' was misunderstood or ignored, Toomer buried the history behind the writing of *Cane* and thereby distorted the book's meaning" (108). What Toomer distorted, as I demonstrate in this chapter, was the degree to which *Cane* and *Holiday*—two books whose lyric, political, and artistic resonance depended on their evocation of lynching—resulted from racial and artistic exchange, on Toomer's "passing for white" as much as on Frank's "passing for black." In the details of their history, particularly their emerging friendship, their trip through the South, their break, and their autobiographical reconstruction of each other, one finds the complexity of racial exchange.

Jean Toomer first met Waldo Frank in 1919, during a trip to New York that Toomer devoted to establishing literary acquaintances. Frank's stature at that time ought not be underestimated: Alan Trachtenberg has noted that "at one time his name stood for the radical cultural and aesthetic aspirations of a whole generation of writers" (viii) and Toomer

---

8. The most noteworthy example of misinformation that has been institutionalized as historical truth is Darwin T. Turner's explanatory footnote in *The Wayward and the Seeking*: "It is important to observe that Toomer states that he had completed *Cane* before Frank completed *Holiday*." This is not true. See Scruggs and VanDemarr's chaps. 4 and 5, in particular, for further elaboration. They demonstrate that "the 1922 correspondence between the two men shows in some detail the central role Frank played in *Cane*'s creation—and not only as critic and editor" (109). Another important and incorrect anecdote connected to this is Toomer's charge that it was in Washington prior to their trip to Spartanburg that he explained his racial "actuality" to Frank: "I read to him 'The First American.' I explained my actuality and my ideas to the point where I felt sure he understood them." Here, too, Toomer is misleading, for Frank had long since read and commented on "The First American" for himself. Again, Scruggs and VanDemarr shrewdly conclude: "Toomer's memoir tries to depict their discussion about 'race' as direct and unambiguous, but his correspondence with Frank shows their exchange to be much more subtle and circuitous" (108).

sympathized with Frank's 1919 work *Our America* (which Van Wyck Brooks called "the Bible of our generation" [qtd. in Hutchinson, *Harlem* 106]), particularly with its emphatic call for a revalued national identity. Toomer wrote to Frank in 1920, asking for an introduction to Ernest Bloch with whom he was hoping to study music. Yet Waldo Frank's reply, which noted, "you are doubtless, by your own findings, musician, but you have a mind that does not show to disadvantage in writing either" (21 Oct. 1920), also commented positively on a letter of Toomer's that had recently been published in *The Call*. Frank's encouragement must have been welcome to Toomer, who had been writing steadily for two years and was anxious to see his work in print.

A year and a half passed before Toomer resumed the correspondence with Frank as well as with a number of New York writers and editors with whom he hoped to cultivate literary contacts. Toomer's 1922 letters to Frank laud the man he was courting as a mentor. In return, Frank replied with the sort of complimentary affection that must have flattered the twenty-eight-year-old aspiring writer. "Glad I was indeed to hear from you, and to read what you had to say," Frank wrote.

> You are the sort of life one doesn't forget . . nor do you grow dim. . . . Yes: Washington must be a lonely place. . . . But I wonder if you are lonelier than I am here in New York? . . . We must still persevere alone . . all of us, scattered suffering, fighting the pain and the menace of under-nutrition of which you speak. . . . Your letter has helped enormously. I wish I could think I could be of help to you. You are one of those men one must see but once to know that timbre and the truth of. About you at present solitude and silence. Well. [sic] mine is broken mostly by the bile-venting of ugly journalists who hate me with a hate I can never understand. And then letters such a [sic] yours, not changing my silence, but filling it with sweetness. (3 Apr. 1920)

Before a month had passed, Toomer sent Frank a batch of his writing—the sketches that would become *Cane*—and Frank responded to them positively and in generous detail in a letter of 25 April. It was clear, Frank wrote, that Toomer had "a vision" but he asserted that "the Form is not there." He suggested that "the trouble is not with the density and amount of this milieu but with the deadness of its texture." Responding to an early draft of "Kabnis," Frank told Toomer, "you are extremely close to your beginning in this deeply individual genre." Toomer's established white mentor Waldo Frank offered detailed suggestions for refining the texture of *Cane*—a significant fact, given that Toomer's lyric style is generally held to be not only his greatest strength, but also, more important, the aesthetic locus of the work's "blackness." Frank concluded, "I am enormously impressed by the power and fullness and fineness of your Say. . . . A man whose spirit is like yours so high and straight a flame does not need to be told that he has enormous gifts." The multipage response closes, "your friend and brother," an endearment that Toomer seized for the opening of his next letter a week later. The two would address each other as "dear brother" or "brother mine" and with explicit testament to their love for the duration of their friendship.

Frank's plan to visit Toomer in Washington during the spring of 1922 was thwarted by the imminent birth of his son Thomas, but Frank planned another trip to the South in the early fall of that year and invited Toomer along: "I am going to stay there ad [sic] just collect and refresh my thoughts and emotions, the maturity of two trips South these past years. Want to come with me? DO! my love to you." Frank wrote Toomer that he sought "some small town with a typical division of white and black folk" (17 July 1922) because he wanted to gather material for additional chapters—one on the Jew and one on the Negro—to add to *Our America*. He also planned a short novel "full of the songs and calls of the black folk" (24 July 1922). Toomer's enthusiasm for the trip is clearly evident: he immediately planned to curtail his own vacation in Harper's Ferry (where Frank's invitation reached him) and return to his grandmother's home in Washington "and save the money against the coming of fall." Moreover, Toomer elaborated on his understanding of Frank's interest in a rich and resonant immersion in Southern folk culture, offering a detailed meditation on the symbolic and historical significance of Harper's Ferry as a prospective destination. Yet in a curiously contradictory and revealing comment, Toomer mentions to Frank that in Harper's Ferry, "transition between the races is neither [difficult] nor hazardous" (19 July 1922).[9]

An important but often undervalued aspect of Toomer's friendship with

---

9. This statement not only presages the exchange in which Frank will suggest that he go south as a Negro, it also seems to undermine Scruggs and Van DeMarr's assertion that "Toomer didn't address the question of passing to Frank, probably because he expected Frank to recognize his rejection of stark racial divisions" (98). Nevertheless, Scruggs and Van DeMarr's analysis of the trip and the correspondence through which Frank and Toomer planned it is a detailed and shrewd one.

Frank in those early stages was the sense of its emotional exchange. The two men matched each other's sentiments, thoughts, compliments, and narratives letter for letter. Toomer sent Frank the draft of his appeal for subscriptions to *City Block*, which reads, in part: "Perhaps I shall never be able to fully gauge the value of [Waldo Frank's] subsequent unfailing interest and friendship. But this I know: they placed a pillar beneath me at a most crucial time; they were warm hands that reached to me when the world seemed most chill and empty." Frank's response testifies to the intimacy that had long manifested itself explicitly, in tender salutations (brother dear, brother mine) and farewells (my love to you; you are wonderfully dear to me), and implicitly, in the promptness with which each man returned the other's letters. Frank writes: "You have helped me too, Jean. Who can measure the balance one way or the other? My deep concern is, to live up to what you from your own generosity of spirit have put upon me and look to me for. It is hard, but the challenge of your love is good, and I accept it . . For the whole course of my life." These passionate letters reflect a friendship predicated, to a significant extent, on exchange, reciprocity, fluidity.

The idea that Frank travel South as a Negro originated when Toomer pointed out that he couldn't travel as a white man, since his own skin was "nearly black from the sun"—a fact that he clearly perceived to be an advantage to the two (qtd. in Kerman and Eldridge 90). Frank did as well, and his enthusiastic response is worth quoting at length: "Wherever we go, South, of course we go together. If you go as a Negro, can't I also? What is a Negro? Doubtless, if the Southerner could see in my heart my feeling for 'the negro,' my love of his great qualities, my profound [sic] for his trials and respect for the great way he bears them, that Southerner would say 'why you're worse than a nigger' . . . so if you go as a Nero [sic], so go I. . . . P S I have always felt that the only truly Christian people in America are the Negroes. Perhaps, since Christianity is a deep outgrowth of Jewish Thought, and I a Jew, this is why I feel as I do toward them" (n.d.). Toomer's many letters had long since indicated that he shared Frank's racial sensibility and complicate any attempt to see Frank as merely using Toomer's racial experience to his own literary advantage. In earlier discussions, for instance, Frank had written, "I am probably presumptuous to write about the Negro, and particularly since I know you who are creating a new phase of American literature" (26 July 1922), but Toomer quickly replied, "There is no poaching in the domain of pure art" (27 July 1922). One oft-cited reference to Sherwood Anderson bears this out. Toomer writes, "Sherwood Anderson and I have exchanged a few letters. I dont think we will go very far. He limits me to Negro. As an approach, as a constant element (part of a larger whole) of interest, Negro is good. But to try to tie me to one of my parts is surely to loose [sic] me. My own letters have taken Negro as a point, and from there have circled out. Sherwood, for the most part, ignores the circles. . . . There is some natural law that brings things to the men they're fitted for. My stuff has been true in direction. Not Sherwood Anderson . . . you. No one in this country but you my brother" (Dec. 1922). Though it might be easy to view these plans in terms of Frank's interests, the trip to Spartanburg was fortuitous for Toomer as well, for Frank's invitation came just as Toomer had conceived of collecting his poems and sketches and was eager to discuss his title and subheadings.[10]

Both men articulated a belief that Spartanburg joined their work as much as it solidified their friendship. Shortly before they left, Toomer wrote to Frank, "I cannot think of myself as being separated from you in the dual task of creating an American literature, and of developing a public, however large or small, capable of responding to our creations. Those who read and know me, should read and know you" (2 Aug. 1922). The two wrote often and optimistically about the collaborative nature of their respective works, and they hopefully anticipated a joint publication of its

---

10. Another, smaller but equally revealing transaction between them also captures the complicated nature of their relationship. Frank had decided to publish and sell his forthcoming novel *City Block* privately, for he feared that censorship laws would subject his friend and publisher Horace Liveright to prosecution. As Frank and Toomer discussed their trip south, they also discussed *City Block*. To wit, Frank invited Toomer to compile a list of friends and acquaintances in Washington who might be interested in purchasing the work. Was this an exploitative manipulation of friendship? Frank seemed well aware of that possibility when he wrote Toomer, "PLEASE, my dear friend, dont undertake this as you well might because you suspect it is my wish and contrary to your convenience" (26 July 1922). Or was Frank doing Toomer a favor by offering him the opportunity to earn a commission, after noticing Toomer's repeated comments about his own limited funds? Money was an issue between them, as Frank not only sent Toomer advances on the sale of *City Block* but also offered to loan him money to cover traveling expenses, suggested ways to economize while traveling, and recommended him (although unsuccessfully) to a wealthy Mrs. Elbert, hoping to set him up with a benefactor. Moreover, money and intimacy seem curiously intertwined in places. When Toomer sends Frank the letter he has written to solicit subscriptions for *City Block*, Frank seems genuinely touched. "There's a healing in that letter to your friends of which you sent me a copy," he writes. "For the important thing is not the selling of copies . . but the impulse that makes you write that letter." Yet in this same letter, which disputes the measurability of affection, Frank includes a check to cover Toomer's clerical expenses.

proceedings. Correspondences following the trip clearly illustrate that for both men, the journey intensified an intimacy between them that both treasured. Toomer happily reported that his grandmother "is in love" with Frank and is the first of Toomer's friends of whom she wholly approves. Frank responds in kind, regularly sending warm greetings to his grandmother and to Mae Wright, Toomer's putative fiancée. "We understand each other in a way that is beautifully mysterious," Frank wrote (n.d.). And Toomer agreed that Spartanburg "gave us each other as perhaps no other place could" (n.d.).

Exchanges that focused specifically on race revealed a continuation of the intimacy and mutual understanding typical of their most intense correspondence. "Holiday progresses," Frank writes in one undated letter following their trip. "I have written the two introductory parts. Now, in medias res! Hard . . but fun. I find color falls off and quality comes forward. I am inside my folks, white and black, and when occasionally I see the glint of their skins it rather shocks me that so little should mean so much." Toomer's response agrees and underscores the point. "The only time that I think 'Negro,'" he writes:

> is when I want a peculiar emotion which is associated with this name. As a usual thing, I actually do not see differences of color and contour. I see differences of life and experience, and often enough these lead me to physical coverings. But not always, and, from the stand point of conventional criticism, not often enough. I'm very satisfied with a character whose body one knows nothing of.
>
> It is true: Spartanburg (how curiously, painfully creative is the South!) gave us each other perhaps as no other place could. A bond that is sealed in suffering endures. And one finger of life can do more weaving than a thousand spindles of literary buzz-buzz.[11]

Frank offered to introduce Toomer to various magazine editors and he encouraged Horace Liveright to publish *Cane*. In early January 1923, the publisher accepted and Frank's mentorship continued as he advised

---

11. Part of my argument here is both contained in and supported by my presentation of the order of their correspondences, several of which were undated. I am implicitly arguing, for example, that the Toomer letter cited here ("The only time that I think 'Negro'") is Toomer's direct response to the Frank letter that I cited above ("I find color falls off and quality comes forward").

Toomer in intricate detail about the minutia of copyreading his page proofs, offering suggestions for dealing with copy editors; he continued to encourage him to come to New York insisting, "if there's any way I can help you get to NY I am ready." He also asked Toomer to help him and Liveright in "reaching a possible Negro public for HOLIDAY."[12]

Before Frank brought the manuscript of *Cane* to Liveright, Toomer asked him to write its introduction. Frank accepted the invitation, though he worried that his own literary reputation might damage Toomer's prospective reception: "Tell me frankly: would you rather I dndt [sic] write the intro.? I have so many enemies, brother mine, that perhaps you'd be better off without my own sponsorship. In that case, be frank. Dont misunderstand. I want to do it, but I dont want this pleasure that wd be mine to stand in your way. You are a genius and your success is all I want." Once he composed his piece, he wrote Toomer again, to convey his intentions. "I have been very circumspect in the Foreword," he wrote, explaining that it "is meant for the public and that it is a piece of diplomacy" (n.d.). But after sending it along, Frank worried, because Toomer didn't write for a while. "BROTHER / I'm a bit worried in your silence. Art thou sick? or did my poor little foreword make you sick? I hope, in this later case, you realise that it is an almost impossible task for a person to write a foreword on a subject in which he feels very powerfully. If he writes a real criticism or expresses his true respect for the book, the thing shrieks its outofplaceness within the same cover." But Toomer wrote to note that the slow mails delayed his receipt of the manuscript. When he did remark on Frank's foreword, his response was enthusiastic and grateful:

> Brother, / The one thing I was uneasy about in a foreword was this: that in doing the necessary cataloging and naming etc the very elements which the book does *not* possess would get plastered across its first pages. I was sure of *you*. I knew you could do the thing. You *have*. The facts for a curious public to toss about, are there. But your point of view is so overwhelmingly that of Art that the divisions and parallelings do not obtrude. I get a good feeling from the whole foreword. And from passages . . . and about Kabnis and

---

12. He apologized for the seemingly mercenary goal and explained that the obligations of a wife and newborn (who was battling illnesses which preoccupied Frank's attention) forced him to "think of sales" (n.d.). Such struggles between the conflicting demands of domestic duty and intellectual life appear regularly in Frank's letters, and he often alludes to his own ongoing battles with depression.

about me as a force, personal, artistic, an understanding wells up that raises the general tone far above a superficial diplomacy. Damn! what a job you had. Congratulations, and love, my brother. And THANKS!

All the while, Toomer planned to go to New York to join the literary crowd with whom he was by then corresponding regularly. Because Frank and Margaret Naumberg found themselves preoccupied with their infant, Frank was able to invite Toomer to his Darien, Connecticut, home for only a short visit. Gorham Munson had offered a more open-ended invitation, and his was a more desirable location in the city.[13] Toomer's purportedly electric first meeting with Naumberg took place in early summer 1923.[14] If Frank was aware of or distressed by their attraction, he did not indicate it in his letter to Toomer late in August 1923, which closes with "Love as ever. . . . and I hope . . until soon."

Yet a noticeable shift appears in Toomer's attitude. In early September—after Toomer and Naumberg's meeting, Horace Liveright wrote to Toomer, asking him to revise an autobiographical sketch he had written as part of the promotional material for *Cane,* not only by shortening it, but also in order to sound "a definite note . . . about your colored blood," which he saw as "the real human interest value of your story." In closing, Liveright invites Toomer to dinner. Toomer's lengthy reply—a letter that has often been cited, but rarely quoted in full—begins by asserting, "My racial composition and my position in the world are realities which I alone may determine." Toomer continues, "Feature Negro if you wish, but do not expect me to feature it in advertisements for you. For myself, I have sufficiently featured Negro in *Cane.*" He goes on to explain his syn-

---

13. His offer was, however, held hostage by Hart Crane who had, by that time, long since worn out his welcome as a houseguest who stayed far too long. Eventually, Crane moved on and in May of that year, Toomer moved to New York.

14. A short note from Frank to Toomer suggests that some tension had arisen earlier, however: "Brother / I've been thinking about you and worrying a bit..But have been silent because your silence made me think you wanted it so. / No energy for a real letter. / all my love / Waldo / Not a single copy have I of Cane!" At the end of May, they were making arrangements for Toomer to visit the Franks in Darien, and afterward, Frank wrote: "Dear Brother / I was glad to have you here, but I was worried lest in my very wearied state I prove a rather unsatisfactory companion. I may not in any overt way show it, but I am tired out, and life seems very hard: and I don't feel fit company for such as you. I'm glad you are so understanding. / Good luck and my love, till the next time . . . / Waldo." As I mentioned, Toomer's biographers date the beginning of his affair with Naumberg at early summer 1923.

thetic view of his racial identity, and to explain that though he permits Liveright to emphasize his Negro lineage for the purposes of advertising, he insists on being identified as multiethnic to potential reviewers. This passage is frequently cited as evidence of Toomer's frustration and distance or of Liveright's exploitative intentions. The point that is often left out of references to this letter, however, is this: Toomer concludes his reply by genially accepting Liveright's dinner invitation. One would imagine that a man as affronted and insulted as many critics would deem him to be would hardly wish to socialize with one so offensive.

These unpublished contemporaneous correspondences contradict Toomer's account in his published autobiographical writings, where he insists, "I answered to the effect that, as I was not a Negro, I could not feature myself as one" (127). The difference may be attributable to a lapse in memory, or it may be related to the fact that Toomer wrote the autobiography around the same time of his marriage to a white woman—a marriage that was highly publicized, during a time in which lynching remained a looming threat to black men who were suspected of relationships with white women. In any case, Toomer's autobiographical version of these events has been accepted as fact.[15] Toomer's assertion that he was betrayed by Liveright is rendered even more questionable by his continued and apparently friendly contact with the publisher. But more than this, Toomer's actions in the 1920s contradicted his autobiographical account of them in the decades following: he actively, demonstrably, and, more to the point, *anonymously* promoted *Cane* and *Holiday* as a sort of "black and white" pair. At Toomer's request, for instance, Liveright tried to arrange for the anonymous publication of Toomer's essay "The South in Literature," a laudatory review that sought to promote sales of both *Cane* and *Holiday* and that frames its analysis by noting that "Waldo Frank is of white, while Jean Toomer is of Negro blood."[16] In another letter to

---

15. David Bradley's essay on Toomer questions, "How . . . could a writer accept so completely in his work what he repudiated in his life?" Bradley agrees that Toomer's "own writings do attest that he was irritated with Horace Liveright's determination to advertise *Cane* as being written by a Negro" (690).

16. Liveright wrote Toomer at the end of September, "Your paper, The South in Literature, is a humdinger and I'm going to take it up with Mr. Messner, the head of our sales department just the best possible way of making use of it. We'll have a copy made of it and we'll send it to Ryan Walker of The Call who I now [sic] will be glad to print it. Of course, as you say, we'll have to sign it with a faked name."

Frank, Toomer hints that he has been thinking about his next book and imagines it as "tremendous." He explains a vision "of the whole brown and black world heaving upward against, here and there mixing with the white world." He writes to Liveright of this vision as well, using precisely the same language.

When Naumberg headed to Reno for a divorce in March 1924, Toomer accompanied her and they lived there together, but they hid this fact carefully. In fact, Toomer orchestrated an elaborate plot in which he asked his elderly grandmother to conceal his whereabouts from all inquirers. What is clear is that once Toomer and Naumberg became intimate, Toomer's attitude toward Frank altered considerably, while Frank's letters maintained a friendly and even tone. The only hint of conflict appears in his response to Toomer's aforementioned essay, "The South in Literature," in which Frank notes "If there were anything to quarrel with you about, I'd do it cordially." He continues, "Your opening paragraph *suggests* that in your opinion there is no meeting ground between my reality in Holiday and the reality which exists fundamentally in the South. I know you do not say this, and you do not believe it. But in your omission of the opposite, there is suggestion of this. And I regret it, because practically all the critics are jumping on me for not knowing the South, and you are the one man who knows I do, who was in a position to state so with some authority." This seems to indicate that it was Toomer who betrayed Frank—both personally and professionally—and not the other way around. Toomer's letters to other literary friends become dismissive of Frank's talent, and his exchanges with Gorham Munson and Margaret Naumberg become increasingly preoccupied with Frank's personal and literary shortcomings.[17]

By contrast, one of Frank's final letters to Toomer comes from France

---

17. In one instance he notes, "I have become a bit stale on Frank criticism," and one of his love letters to Margaret includes a petty description of how Frank once misrepresented Toomer's initial impressions of Gorham Munson to Munson—a distortion that seems to Toomer to be "evidence . . . of the hard road ahead." Gorham Munson and his wife Lisa were manifestly caught up in the triangle created by Toomer and Naumberg's affair. In responding to Toomer's apparent pressure that he choose sides, Munson resists, noting, "One side has been explicit but *not complete* in its testimony: the other side has not uttered a word." He continued, noting his anguish: "I have been grieved at different times at the manner in which you have identified yourself with various 'spiritual' movements and have always created an opposition between these movements and Waldo."

in February—and would have arrived just as Toomer was planning his secret trip to Reno where he would live with Naumberg. The letter is worth reproducing in full:

> Dear Jean:
>
> I wish you would write to me, and tell me why you left New York the way you did, and why you did not answer the letter I wrote to you on my departure: and tell me what you have been doing and what is going on in your soul, your mind, your life.
>
> I have been away nearly four months. I have thought much of you, and waited patiently for a letter. I have had no word. Did you possible [sic] write, and was your letter lost? I know that such things happen. I know nothing by way of news of you save an occasional mention by Gorham who says he sees you little, by Hart who says likewise and that you are meditating much, and by Margaret who mentioned your presence at a party of Paul's one evening on MacDougal Street to dinner..That is the exact sum of my knowledge, of you. Do you think that is just? I am your friend / Waldo

Frank takes on the tone of a jilted lover here, and his appeal for a return to intimacy and connection clearly contain homoerotic elements that only serve to underscore the sense of betrayal of which Toomer—not Frank—seems guilty. But that sense of betrayal can only be recognized by readers who know where Toomer was when Frank wrote it, and too few readers or critics know this.[18] A full and honest reading of correspondence between Toomer and Frank thus illustrates how the cynicism and oversimplification of our own attitudes toward race and power can obscure a full understanding of literary influence. Toomer's self-serving charge that Frank betrayed him worked well because it fit neatly into the belief that racial power supersedes all other kinds of power. Ironically,

---

18. Siobhan Somerville's excellent analysis of the parallel discourses of racial segregation and normative sexuality in the early twentieth century argues that such compulsory heterosexuality "has drawn much of its ideological power from the ways in which it buttresses as well as depends on naturalized categories of racial difference" (137). Her analysis of Toomer's autobiographical writings demonstrates their ability to challenge normative categories of race and masculinity. But she too reads Toomer's unpublished writings and his correspondences with Frank through the sort of sympathetic perspective that tends to view Toomer as a victim of Frank's machinations, arguing, for instance, that "Frank's own racial envy and desire later shaped his representation of Toomer as a 'Negro' writer to publishers and other writers, an emphasis on racial identity that Toomer resisted and that brought irreparable tension to the surface of their relationship" (160).

however, this is precisely the ideology that Jean Toomer would spend his life's work battling. By charging Frank and Liveright with a mercenary and selfish desire to exploit his racial identity, Jean Toomer painted himself into an even darker ideological corner.

Toomer's ungallant behavior may reflect his individualism, but it also offers an implicit critique of unrestrained individualism. The point of this discussion is not to present Toomer as a model for the liberating potential of race passing—indeed, when one considers the shallowness and selfishness of his actions, one is left with a distinctly skeptical attitude toward the man and his life's choices. But the reasons for such skepticism differ dramatically from those articulated by race conscious and ideologically driven critics like Alice Walker, who promotes an essentialist view of Toomer's talent—in order to claim *Cane* as a work of black artistic genius—but an antiessentialist view of his life itself. Indeed, in examining the contrasting responses to Jean Toomer and to the Ex-Colored Man, one is struck by the critical predisposition to think the very best of the former and the very worst of the latter. Perhaps the contrasting legacies result from the Ex-Colored Man's having kept evidence of his talent private, those "fast yellowing manuscripts" remaining as invisible as the evidence of his black identity; Toomer's *Cane*, by contrast, offered public evidence of his blackness, even though that blackness was not obvious to the unknowing observer.

5 | Passing and the Rise of Mass Culture

Jessie Fauset, the most prolific woman novelist of the Harlem Renaissance, believed that good literature contains and conveys "the universality of experience." In a 1922 letter to then fledgling writer Jean Toomer, she encourages him to read the classics in order to find "the same reaction to beauty, to love, to freedom. It gives you a tremendous sense of ful-ness [sic], and completeness, a linking up of your life with others like yours." But the cultural and social changes of the 1920s curtailed the possibility of precisely the sort of meaningful connection that Fauset advocates. Jessie Fauset wrote to Jean Toomer with optimism and conviction, believing—as did her mentor W. E. B. Du Bois—in the potential of beautiful art to bridge political divides; yet she encouraged Toomer to find community in a world that was fast becoming a place of alienation and estrangement, and she sent Toomer straight into the arms of that world. "You've got personality and no prejudicing appearances," she noted. "Why not try to break into the newspaper game in one of the big cities?" As Fauset's own fiction makes clear, the "newspaper game" both caused and reflected the fragmented nature of urban communities.

The potential of art to link lives and form a common ground informs Jessie Fauset's most highly regarded novel, the 1928 bildungsroman *Plum Bun*. Critics have viewed the work as a novel of manners, an investigation of racial liminality, an analysis of gender roles that subvert or restrict female sexuality, and most often, as a pointed critique of protagonist Angela Murray's attempt to pass for white.[1] Yet many, if not all of these analyses turn on presumptions about boundaries that the novel seeks explicitly to undermine. *Plum Bun* is, of course, shaped by the

---

1. See, for instance, Elizabeth Ammons, "New Literary History: Edith Wharton and Jessie Redmon Fauset," *College Literature* 14 (1987): 207–18; Cheryl Wall, *Women of the Harlem Renaissance* (Bloomington: Indiana UP, 1995) 73–79; Deborah McDowell, "The Neglected Dimensions of Jessie Redmon Fauset," *Afro-Americans in New York Life and History* 5 (1981), 33–49; and Ann duCille, *The Coupling Convention* (New York: Oxford UP, 1993).

particularities of Angela Murray's identity and therefore grapples with the material and epistemological constitution of race, class, and gender. But the novel also raises some of the broader philosophical questions that underlie Fauset's advice to Jean Toomer: Does absolute freedom aid or obstruct the development of meaningful identity? Do the values of a clearly defined community inform or limit individuality? Can someone like Jean Toomer or Angela Murray—both of whom struggled to negotiate an organic sense of self apart from the (arbitrary) social categories assigned them—ever find a sense of "fullness" or "completeness"?

Plum Bun, as I demonstrate here, extends and complicates the analysis of identity, citizenship, and the nature of community life taking place in the public discourse of the 1920s—by "linking up" the concerns of the Harlem Renaissance with those of American intellectual culture generally. Such a reading ventures to engage the challenge posed by Ann duCille, who insists, "Critics and theorists of African American literature must conceptualize race, class, culture, and experience, as well as traditions and canons, in terms far less natural, absolute, linear, and homogeneous than we have in the past" (148). To read Fauset in the context of her contemporary intellectual culture, then, is to see more clearly that she was neither anachronistic nor marginal, as early critics charged. In *Plum Bun,* the trope of passing for white raises many of the same issues about the individual and society that animated public debate among prominent intellectuals; and, more pointedly, the novel *racializes* those discussions, thereby revealing the role of race and gender in the debate. Angela Murray's passing for white reflects the multivalent transaction in which white American culture was then participating. Her particular movement from a black identity to a white identity invokes the larger movement—from Victorian morals to modernist ethos, from family to city, from community to individuality, from tradition to self-generation— that characterized a broader American cultural anomie.

The book's title and organization derive from the children's nursery rhyme, "To Market, to Market / To buy a Plum Bun; / Home again, Home again, / Market is done," which is included on the novel's title page. The story focuses on Angela Murray, a young, light-skinned painter who tries, unsuccessfully, to pass for white. She leaves Philadelphia and her younger, darker sister Virginia and moves to New York as the white Angele Mory, ostensibly to study drawing. In New York, she meets two men: Anthony Cross, a quiet and passionate and poor artist who loves her; and Roger Fielding, a rich white boy whom she considers her ticket to wealth and freedom. Eventually Virginia decides to move to New York as well and agrees to keep Angela's racial secret. But on the day Jinny arrives, Roger Fielding appears unexpectedly at the train station, and to safeguard her own racial reputation and maintain Roger's affection Angela pretends not to know her sister and abandons her. The sisters ultimately reunite, and Angela brings an end to her passing by announcing her "true racial identity" to a roomful of newspaper reporters in support of a fellow art student, a black woman. Angela then travels to Paris to study art and in the novel's last line is reunited with Anthony, whose multiracial identity has since been revealed and who has long been understood to be Angela's true love.

Even before Angela passes for white, numerous references encourage readers of *Plum Bun* to view her as a quintessential American individualist: she is born in Philadelphia at the turn of the century, for example, into a family whose sentimental relations are directly influenced by such encroaching industrial developments as washing machines and automobiles. Indeed, the problems she finds in self-definition are exacerbated by the cultural transformations following the Great War, transformations that influence her status as black and as a woman. When Angela moves to New York as the white Angele Mory, therefore, she cannot distinguish between her perceived absolute freedom and a more elusive meaningful liberty; and when Angela betrays and abandons her sister at the train station, Fauset explores the consequences of her protagonist's radical individualism. The implications for citizenship are clear, as Angela discovers that a meaningful personal identity depends on a strong connection with a sympathetic community. Clear, too, are the implications for literary production. Ann duCille has noted the instability of form in Fauset's novels, arguing that "Fauset is indeed writing neither realism nor naturalism; nor is she falling back on pure romanticism. She is interrogating old forms and inventing something new" (100). In *Plum Bun*, Angela's rejection of her sister and her race analogize generic transition because she has left a home that vividly evokes nineteenth-century domestic fiction. In this evocation, Fauset simultaneously engages and critiques the racial dimensions of the mythology of American literature and specifically its presentation of the American dream.

Even before the Great War destroyed the faith of white Americans in their own inviolability, Walter Lippmann's 1914 *Drift and Mastery* gave voice to the same sense of cultural ennui that Angela experiences. "We have changed our environment more quickly than we know how to change ourselves" (92), he writes in a chapter whose title, "A Big World and Little Men," anticipates Angela's entrance to New York, in which "Fifth Avenue is a canyon; its towering buildings dwarf the importance of the people hurrying through its narrow confines." (87). Lippmann argues that religious authority has been undermined by the advent of scientific thought, that big business has rendered political systems inefficient, and that a sense of community has become increasingly fragmented. As a result, he concludes, life's "impersonal quality is intolerable: people don't like to deal with abstractions" (93). For Americans in all regions—but particularly for those in urban centers like New York—the war exacerbated this sense of alienation. Jessie Fauset privately encouraged Jean Toomer to discover "the universality of experience" in a world where the sheer enormity of "the war to end all wars" demanded that nations recognize their membership in a global community. John Dewey's postwar analysis *The Public and Its Problems* likened the war's spread to "an uncontrolled natural catastrophe. The consolidation of peoples in enclosed, nominally independent, national states has its counterpart in the fact that their acts affect groups and individuals in other states all over the world" (128). In shattering the boundaries by which countries defined themselves, the First World War also ruptured those boundaries by which individual identities acquired clarity and stability.

The two decades following the Great War saw dramatic alterations in how white Americans thought about personal identity. Ann Douglas has demonstrated with telling detail how the war created what she terms "the culture of momentum." Profound material, political, philosophical, and epistemological changes wrought by the war irrevocably quickened the pace of modern life. "As Gertrude Stein pointed out," Douglas notes, "in a period of immense change like that of the Great War, fast assimilation is a prerequisite for power; the country least hampered by past conventions and traditions, least subject to cultural lag, most oriented toward the future, most alert to incentives to modernize, will dominate" (87). The appeal of Herbert Hoover, elected just before *Plum Bun* was published, lay in his being an engineer and in his presenting himself as a modern man who could both understand and control the technological forces then at work. It was not just the production of Henry Ford automobiles that was affected by modern technology, but also the transmission of information and the reproduction and presentation of images. The increased availability of telephones, telegraphs, newspapers, movies, and radios made communication cheap and easy. Likewise, mass-produced food, clothing, toiletries, household appliances, and entertainment made the material conditions of life less demanding. But at what cost, asked intellectuals and cultural critics? To what end? These unsettling developments in material culture and religious authority also converged in the Scopes trial of 1925, in which science and religion battled for legal primacy.[2] In the first jury trial publicly broadcast live on the radio, the drama of Clarence Darrow examining William Jennings Bryan was one that demonstrated not only the power and the limits of rhetoric to persuade, but also the market appeal of philosophical debate. It is precisely this transition—from familiarity to uncertainty, from religious conviction to scientific skepticism, from community to individualism, from nineteenth-century values to twentieth-century promise—that, is metonymized in Angela Murray's passing for white.

In the opening section of *Plum Bun,* "Home," home, race, and sisterhood have already lost their coherence. Early on Angela finds herself disenchanted with her hometown, Philadelphia, the city where the U.S. Constitution was ratified. Twenty-seven years old at the conclusion of the novel, it is little wonder that Angela's birth year corresponds to that of the twentieth century. The motif of transition figures into all aspects of her character, as Angela finds herself wholly disillusioned with the small, closed, rigidly restricted domestic sphere that just one generation earlier epitomized comfort and success. But her sense of rebellion is determined by her character rather than by her chronological age, as we see in the contrast between Angela and her younger sister. Virginia, who fully accepts a black racial identity, thoroughly embraces her parents' old-fashioned, sentimental, and parochial traditions. Her name evokes more than just her virginal innocence, though that evocation certainly resonates: Virginia's values derive from the slave culture of the old South;

---

2. In the so-called Monkey Trial of 1925, Dayton, Tennessee, high school teacher John T. Scopes was charged with violating a state law that prohibited teaching evolution. The case, which gained widespread publicity and was nationally broadcast by radio, was prosecuted by William Jennings Bryan; Clarence Darrow defended Scopes and was supported by the American Civil Liberties Union.

her ostensibly sweet and gentle demeanor belies her deeper strength, and ultimately she reveals herself to be shrewdly cunning. Different skin colors—Angela's whiteness and Jinny's "rosy bronzeness" (14)—may have predisposed the sisters to their different characters or they may have simply accentuated the differences that already existed. In *Plum Bun*, the racial significance of the differences between the sisters is further complicated because Angela, the older sister, shuns the ideology of domesticity that Jinny, the younger sister, embraces. And both reject predestination, suggesting that some generational upheaval has ruptured the flow of progress. Older and introspective, Angela craves independence, looks forward; young and vivacious, Jinny craves domesticity, looks backward. Virginia's character thus aligns the notion of a small, intimate, organic community with its literary archetype, the sentimental novel. Religious devotion binds Virginia to her family, and Christian faith binds the family to its community.

Allusions to literary traditions frame references to social traditions in the novel's first half, where it becomes clear that Virginia's belief in the power of family is deepened and sustained by her religious devotion. The hyperbolic language with which Fauset describes this attachment establishes Virginia's sensibilities as deeply entrenched in the sentimental tradition: "She loved the atmosphere of golden sanctity which seemed to hover with a sweet glory about the stodgy, shabby little dwelling" (20). This "sweet glory" calls Virginia to a life of domestic service rendered noble in its devotion to God and family. The first page of the "Home" section describes how, by twelve years of age, Virginia had discovered the pleasures of housekeeping. She "had already developed a singular aptitude and liking for the care of the house," and she fulfilled "all the duties of Sunday morning"—housecleaning, cooking breakfast, waking and serving the family, entertaining them by playing the piano as they dress for church—chores in which she "found a nameless and sweet satisfaction" (20). Virginia is so deeply and continually affected by this ritual of servitude that, after breakfast, when she played religious hymns that her parents sang with her, the "little girl" experienced "a sensation of happiness which lay perilously near tears" (21).

Religious services conjure a reaction so intense in Virginia as to evoke sexuality. Virginia experiences communion services as spiritually sensual; the description of these services resembles orgasm: "In the exquisite diction of the sacramental service there were certain words, certain phrases that almost made the child faint; the minister had a faint burr in his voice and somehow this lent a peculiar underlying resonance to his intonation; he half spoke, half chanted and when, picking up the wafer he began 'For in the night' and then broke it, Virginia could have cried out with the ecstasy which filled her" (23). Virginia is, significantly, too young to participate in this ritual of consummation, here rendered multi-faceted and multiply suggestive, but she senses its importance by observing those who do. Taking communion seems to "transfigure" people; her parents, it seems, "wore an expression of ineffable content as they returned to their seats" (23). In this interconnection of religious fervor, displaced sexuality, and consumption, Jessie Fauset not only draws together the most powerful themes of her literary ancestors, she also delineates the cultural transition in which the authority of religion will give way to the emerging complexity and prominence of modernity.

Such an analogy problematizes literature's role in defining race, in creating ideological stereotypes by which we order the world. Certainly Virginia evokes the literary heroines of black women's fiction, so-called tragic mulattoes like Iola Leroy who maintain race-conscious fidelity to "her people." But to recognize that many of Virginia's literary ancestors are white girl heroines of nineteenth-century romances and domestic fictions is to acknowledge that *Plum Bun* cannot easily be located generically or in terms of its racial ideology.[3] Though the narrative explicitly draws our attention to Angela, the obvious protagonist, Virginia operates as a background foil, a figure who recalls, critiques, and at times deconstructs the literary tradition and social history against which Angela seeks to define herself. It is not only the black women's convention that operates in this polarity but the canonical tradition as well. One could argue that Nathaniel Hawthorne's echo also sounds in Virginia's characterization: the romanticization of domestic labor by which Fauset defines Virginia was a strategy employed in *The House of the Seven Gables* in order to

---

3. Even among theoretically and ideologically like-minded critics, disagreement reigns: Hazel Carby argues that "ultimately the conservatism of Fauset's ideology dominates her texts" (*Reconstructing* 167), whereas Ann duCille finds criticism that dismisses Fauset for her ostensible celebration of light skin and marriage to be "ahistorical in the degree to which [such critics] chide early African American writers for not being 100 to 150 years ahead of their times [and condemn writers like Fauset] for writing through and against the dominant racial and sexual ideologies of their times, rather than out of the enlightened, feminist vision of ours" (18).

reconstitute women's work as pleasure, not labor. In fact, Carolyn Wedin Sylvander sees Hawthorne's influence in the narrative structuralization that incorporates the nursery rhyme motif into the novel form. "The pattern of romance as Nathaniel Hawthorne developed it in *The House of the Seven Gables,* departure and return, or isolation to communion, is thus put into child's verse," Sylvander argues. "By adopting the freedoms of the American romance for formal structure, Fauset is able to accomplish a whole series of aims in *Plum Bun*" (184). As a figure redolent of nineteenth-century ideology, Virginia also evokes the literary tradition in which, as Michael T. Gilmore has argued, the middle class emerged in all of its potential and confusion. "Nathaniel Hawthorne," he notes, "maps the emergence of the middle class and simultaneously reveals the self-contradictory and unsettled nature of the new configuration" ("Hawthorne" 216). Through Virginia's traditional femininity, Fauset folds this class consciousness into a gendered role: her middle-class virtue defines the community against which Angela rebels. In the opening "Home" section of *Plum Bun,* then, Virginia's characterization locates several nebulous historical, cultural, and literary transitions. It evokes the formulation and simultaneous instability of the middle class; it subsumes personal identity into a vacuous romantic stereotype (a critique of which will become evident in her move to New York and eventual cosmopolitanism); and it establishes—in order to critique it—a dialectic of opposition as the bifurcated paradigm through which Angela must assert her own identity.

The sentimental trope that Jinny seems to personify was often used by the generation of black women writers who preceded Fauset; these women presented the domestic ideal in order to affirm community and family as sites where women have social and civic presence. Claudia Tate has argued persuasively that "the idealized domesticity in these novels [functioned] as a fundamental symbol of the Victorian era for representing civil ambition and prosperity as a nineteenth-century 'metonym for proper social order,' a symbol that black women writers in particular used to promote the social advancement of African Americans" (*Domestic* 5). But for all of its apparent and romanticized appeal, the ideology of domesticity, as it is incorporated into Virginia's young self, contains the very elements of its own undoing. This "blessed 'Sunday feeling'" (20) that affects Virginia so deeply has resounding political implications, for her sensibility is both wholly satisfied and portends cultural stagnation: "She envied no one the incident of finer clothes or a larger home; this unity was the core of happiness, all other satisfactions must radiate from this one; greater happiness could only be a matter of degree but never of essence. When she grew up she meant to marry a man exactly like her father and she would conduct her home exactly like her mother" (22). The incestual undertones in Virginia's wish to marry a man like her father hint at her desire to thwart social evolution by replicating her parents' lives rather than surpassing them. Notwithstanding her ambition "to invent a marvellous method for teaching the pianoforte" (13), Virginia feels none of the desire to succeed that fuels social change or political progress.

In *Plum Bun,* explicit invocations of literary genre frame Angela's decision to pass for white, aligning her rejection of blackness with a rejection of the sentimental tradition of domestic fiction. Angela has little regard for the sentiments that define Virginia's world. "She did not like going to church, at least not to their church, but she did care about her appearance and she liked the luxuriousness of being 'dressed up' on two successive days" (21). Being "dressed up" and attending to her appearance is, in fact, Angela's single greatest pleasure. The narrator tells us that "Saturday came to be the day of the week for Angela" (20) because this is the day on which "Angela learned the possibilities for joy and freedom which seemed to her inherent in mere whiteness" (14). Angela associates the white world with a particular kind of freedom, however: she is happiest when idle and on display. Her most satisfied Saturdays consist of shopping, lunching, and attending the orchestra.

To Angela and her mother Mattie, "a successful and interesting afternoon" consists of making a virtue of their uselessness and of continual self-objectification: "They had browsed among the contents of the small exclusive shops in Walnut Street; they had had soda at Adams' on Broad Street and they were standing finally in the portico of the Walton Hotel deciding with fashionable and idle elegance what they should do next" (18). For Mattie, these afternoons offer an escape from class as much as race, and they teach Angela to embrace the luxuries of consumer culture. A romantic and an idealist, Mattie wanted her daughters to become great artists; her sensible husband Junius overrode that wish, however, and insisted on giving the girls "a good, plain education." But Junius's protective devotion to Mattie also indulged her love for material culture. The demands of Mattie's work week create the pleasure of her Saturdays: "all innocent, childish pleasures pursued without malice or envy contrived to

cast a glamour over Monday's washing and Tuesday's ironing, the scrub-
bing of the kitchen and bathroom and the fashioning of children's
clothes" (16). Angela experiences the public pleasures of the marketplace's gratification individually, selfishly, and she fails to see its broader
communal effects; at the same time, she has inadvertently learned to con-
flate an artistic sensibility with material comfort.

Angela's predisposition to view fate, rather than God, as primarily responsible for her life's path most clearly and pointedly distinguishes her
as representative of nascent twentieth-century thought. By arguing that
"merit is not always rewarded" (12), *Plum Bun* racializes the nineteenth-
century mythology that popularized Horatio Alger's apocryphal tales of
fantastic "rags to riches" success. Angela frames her desire for independence—"Freedom! That was the note which Angela heard oftenest in the
melody of living which was to be hers" (13)—wholly in terms of race. The
family ties that Jinny treasures mean little to Angela. Her outright rejection of Jinny, the sharpest consequence of passing, is precipitated by "a
faint pity" she feels "for her unfortunate relatives" with dark skin (18).
Likewise, Angela finds nothing appealing in the company of neighbors
and friends who make, for Virginia, an essential community. Angela finds
Matthew Henson, a potential beau, to be "insufferably boresome and
[she] made no effort to hide her ennui" (24). She responds to Jinny's piano playing "in sheer self-defense"—she leaves the room to eat supper
alone rather than experience the emotions that her sister's religious music might evoke.

It is an important part of her story that Angela experiences both her
greatest satisfaction and her most painful racial rejection in her beloved
art class. Even though her teachers assure her that she'll "find artistic folk
the broadest, most liberal people in the world" (65), they cut her coldly
when they learn of her racial lineage. The novel conjoins this rebuff with
a similar, more public humiliation at the movie theater, and Angela's bitterness about these rejections grows more cynical in the face of her sister's calm acceptance. Angela's decision to pass emerges from such moments of pointed confusion. How can Jessie Fauset's personal advice to
Jean Toomer and her public advocation of an "art" that serves racial justice reconcile with these fictional depictions? In Philadelphia, Angela's
development as an artist is continually circumscribed by the fact of her
race—by her invisible blood—and not, importantly, by the appearance
of racial difference. Angela utterly rejects the community-oriented,

racially loyal, and sentimentally genteel realm embraced by her sister. When a friend suggests that racial experience enhances artistic growth, Angela responds with brutal frankness: "'Oh, don't drag me into your old discussion,' she says crossly. 'I'm sick of this whole race business if you ask me. . . . No, I don't think being coloured in America is a beautiful thing. I think it's nothing short of a curse'" (53). Angela's cynical realism countermands her sister's domesticity. Sharing more attributes with fictional contemporaries like Jay Gatsby and Lily Bart than the likes of Megda or Clotel, Angela strives to become the fully individualized product of her own imagination.[4]

The racialized contrast between (dark) Jinny's embrace of tradition and (light) Angela's desire for freedom plays out against a background specifically inscribed with America's postwar cultural transitions. The Murray household has been influenced—and its familial relationships altered—by the same encroaching tensions and technologically induced displacements that many intellectuals were then lamenting. Washing day—once a ritual that reinforced the connections between home and work life, wherein Junius "tried to work uptown so that he could run in and help Mattie"—evolves as the girls grow up. When they were young, their father "used to run in two or three time [sic] in the course of a morning to lend a hand." But this ceremony is irrevocably altered with "the advent of the washing machine" (33). Though the workload, to be sure, is reduced, the communal chore also is dissolved and reduced to a "pleasant fiction" (33). Leisurely Saturday afternoons also become a thing of the past. During the girls' childhoods, Saturdays were days of enormous pleasure when Mattie and Angela would go shopping while Junius and Virginia toured the city; but by their adulthood, the "Saturday excursions were long since a thing of the past; Henry Ford had changed that" (56). As the sisters grow older and begin working as teachers, the family becomes increasingly fragmented and communal time dissipates; eventually, not even church services bring them together.

Plum Bun thus records cultural instability and writes race into its

---

4. In aligning Angela with fictional white protagonists Jay Gatsby, of F. Scott Fitzgerald's 1925 *The Great Gatsby*, and Lily Bart, from Edith Wharton's 1905 *The House of Mirth*, I mean to suggest that Angela shares their insistence on self-determination and self-realization. By contrast, important black title characters such as Emma Dunham Kelley's 1891 Megda, and William Wells Brown's 1853 Clotel emphasize community values like loyalty and humility.

account. The novel's structuralization underscores this dissonance through its unlikely juxtaposition of nursery rhyme and marketplace. *Plum Bun* the novel critiques the white bias in "Plum Bun" the nursery rhyme by removing it from the nursery and projecting it into an adult, market-driven sphere. Its five sections, "Home," "Market," "Plum Bun," "Home Again," and "Market Is Done," reveal transactions not anticipated in the nursery rhyme.[5] By positing a nursery rhyme motif, Fauset critiques the literary form through which cultural indoctrination into class and race consciousness occurs; her use of "Plum Bun" highlights the nursery rhyme's assumption that selfhood finds expression—and, indeed, children find happiness—through acquisition and consumption. "Plum Bun" the nursery rhyme simplifies its manifestations of value and exchange; *Plum Bun* the novel complicates them. "Plum Bun" celebrates the movement linking homes and marketplaces; *Plum Bun* critiques them.

In the twentieth century's marketplace of values, Angela sells her family in order to buy her freedom: "Her plan was to sell the house and divide the proceeds. With her share of this and her half of the insurance she would go to New York or Chicago, certainly to some place where she could by no chance be known, and launch out 'into a freer, fuller life'" (80). But with Angela's sale of real estate, Fauset invests in what Ann duCille terms "unreal estate," a fantastic fictional realm that combines the historically specific and the sentimental. In this "ideologically charged space," black writers ranging from William Wells Brown to Ann

---

5. Numerous critics have noted the nursery-rhyme motif through which *Plum Bun* is titled and ordered, though they have read that motif to different ends. Joseph J. Feeney argues that the nursery rhyme offers an ironic counterstructure through which Fauset exposes "the anger, the tragedy, the sardonic comedy, the disillusioned hopes, the bitterness against white Americans" felt by black Americans ("Sardonic" 367). The "Plum Bun" nursery rhyme in particular, Feeney notes, resonates with the reminder that "only whites go to market, only whites enjoy a plum bun" ("Black Childhood" 69). In addition, Deborah McDowell's feminist reading of the fairy-tale motif in Fauset's 1924 novel *There Is Confusion* and her story "The Sleeper Wakes" offers a useful perspective. McDowell argues that "Fauset was aware of how folk literature—particularly fairy tales—serves to initiate the acculturation of children to traditional social roles, expectations and behaviors, based on their sex" ("Neglected" 35). Thus, enacting the fairy tale critiques the fairy tale. In McDowell's reading, Fauset summarily undermines the fairy tale's implicit ideology: "'Happily-ever-after' is not marriage to a handsome, wealthy prince but realization and acceptance of the virtues of the black cultural experience as well as a realization and rejection of conventional social relationships that are injurious to the growth of selfhood" (38).

Petry have fictionally embroidered historical facts, duCille, argues, "usually for decidedly political purposes" (18). Even as Angela ostensibly rejects her African American *racial* heritage, therefore, Jessie Fauset claims her African American *literary* heritage. The opening section of *Plum Bun*, aptly titled "Home," concludes by depicting the real-estate transaction in which Jinny purchases sole proprietorship of the family's home and history from Angela, who consigns her name, her race, and her past. But in the second, equally well-titled "Market" section, Angela enters into a world of "unreal estate," where sculptor Augusta Savage appears in the disguise of Miss Powell and W. E. B. Du Bois seems embodied in the fictional Van Meier.

When Angela moves to New York, she encounters the pseudo-environment created by an increasingly volatile and mechanized mass society. New York is a city where, as Walter Lippmann argues, "what each man does is based not on direct and certain knowledge, but on pictures made by himself or given to him" (*Drift* 25). Indeed, New York is a marketplace rather than a home, and Angela's familial irresponsibility translates into financial irresponsibility that is most evident in her housing decisions. Her new friend Paulette marvels at Angela's naive choice of lodging. "In a hotel?" she exclaims, as Angela blushes in embarrassment. "In Union Square? Child, are you a millionaire? Where did you come from? Don't you care anything about the delights of home?" (99). From the start, Fauset makes it clear that Angela's inability to capitalize on the exchange rate of white skin parallels her unfortunate miscalculation of the meaning of home.

In New York, Angela mistakes alienation for independence; moreover, she discovers that while whiteness imparts absolute freedom, such freedom does not guarantee a meaningful identity. Instead, because she views freedom as an end in itself rather than as a means to an end—that is, as a means to establishing a rewarding identity—her experience of freedom is characterized by estrangement, drift, and alienation. Her aimless wandering—"she was becoming unconscionably idle" (91)—evinces this loss of subjectivity, and her idleness reinforces her lack of social connections. Angela's arrival in New York and her simultaneous passing for white thus reflect a transition from an identifiable community into an undifferentiated mass society and thereby illustrates the consequences of a world John Dewey described in 1927, a world in which "no amount of aggregated collective action of itself constitutes a community" (151).

Angela's removal to New York also depicts the tensions identified by German sociologist Ferdinand Tonnies, whose 1887 work on community and society demonstrates how communities grow from acts of will, rather than from organic, inherent conditions. Tonnies raises questions that Fauset engages through Angela, and both demonstrate that community, which is an extension of family, faces difficult challenges in a world in which family life is decaying.

In New York, Angela Mory wants to create herself by associating with a sympathetic and like-minded community. But first, she finds pleasant distraction at the movies, where she now "found herself studying the screen with a strained and ardent intensity" (91). Her attraction to performance reinforces both her new name and her claim to New York, for as Ann Douglas observes, "Constructed identity is at bottom an affair of masks and role playing, part of the politics of theatricality" (344). Angela's easy access to movies and theaters reflects white New York's desire to be entertained and its lack of interest in direct political action. Readily available mass-produced movies sought profit over artistic merit, and genre pictures used assembly-line strategies to keep audiences enthralled. The initial success of Angela's own performance—her passing for white—predisposes her to accept the cinema's formulaic fictions without question, and she loses "the slight patronizing skepticism" that characterized her previous critical judgment (91). But her loss of discriminating individuality is exacerbated by a palling loneliness, and in her favorite theater, Angela often watches the audience more than the play, noting the intimate groups in attendance. In this way, her experience demonstrates an emerging truth about mass culture: Angela joins the mass culture simply by attending a performance, but as a member of the audience, she merely watches the show in the dark; alienated and unconnected, her membership has no significant value.

If Angela's experience as an anonymous spectator at the theater undermines her critical perceptions, her parallel experience as a spectator in the world, by contrast, nourishes her artistic growth. As a spectator in the world, an observer of human behavior and of the human face, Angela becomes an artist. Jessie Fauset thus offers her protagonist the same opportunity for connection that she encouraged in Jean Toomer—"a linking up of your life with others like yours." Once independent, Angela finds herself drawn to the very same sort of intimacy and security that she rejected at home. Her expectation that whiteness and freedom would bring rewards gives way to the ironic realization that they only bring expense. Her initial weeks of residence in New York are marked both by her sense of adventure and by that adventure's cost: "She had been in New York eight months and she had already spent a thousand dollars. At this rate her little fortune which had seemed at first inexhaustible would last her less than two years" (110). Friendships involve expenditure in New York: she is beholden to her comrades for lunches, teas, gifts. And though the price of these socials adds up, the emotional rewards are less congruous: Miss Powell responds to her with an "attitude of dignified reserve" (108); Paulette "lived in a state of constant defiance" (112); and Martha Burden "was cool and slightly aloof" (112). These ostensible sisters share an understanding of the world, insights that are alien to Angela. Human interaction is regulated and commodified in this artificially constructed community, and the synthetic nature of Angela's friendships underscores the alienation of urban life.

Despite this, it does appear that Angela is gifted with painterly insights. In Harlem, she sees aesthetic possibilities in a world shaped by art. "A man's sharp, high-bred face etched itself on her memory," Fauset notes, "—the face of a professional man, perhaps,—it might be an artist" (96). The language here posits the man's face as the agent of artistic etching, not Angela. The intimation that blackness inscribes itself as artistic vision onto Angela is underscored when Fauset tells us that Angela sees Harlem as "fuller, richer, not finer but richer with the difference in quality that there is between velvet and silk" (98). But still, she rejects the intense devotion and potential happiness in Anthony's love because it involves commitment: she "wanted none of Anthony's poverty and privation and secret vows . . . to REAL ART" (143).

The contrast between Roger and Anthony further underscores how Angela misunderstands the meaning of freedom. She believes that Anthony's poverty will restrict her, when in fact it is Roger's prosperity (and the obligations to his father that accompany it) that brings the greatest demands. Contrary to Angela's belief that Roger represents freedom, his presence in her life proves far more inhibiting than liberating. In ironic juxtaposition to his wealth, she amasses "a little heap" of bills in the process of their affair because "she had had to dress to keep herself dainty and desirable" for him (151). Martha Burden advises Angela to manipulate Roger in order to extract a marriage proposal. Thereafter, most of her actions are contrived: she views the relationship as a game in which she "decided to follow all the rules as laid down by Martha Burden and to add any workable ideas of her own" (146). Rather than affording her the opportunity to develop a full and meaningful identity, Angela's relationship with Roger only stifles her. Roger's financial independence cannot even help him to establish a meaningful identity for himself—for all of his advantages, he proves to be shallow, small-minded, and intimidated. His behavior in orchestrating the eviction of the black patrons from a restaurant disproves Angela's belief that he "had no fears, no restraints, no worries" (129). He defers so wholly to his father's wishes that he has no independent character: "I'm not entirely my own master," he explains (185). Echoing the terms of Lippmann's *Drift and Mastery,* Roger articulates the sense of dislocation that characterizes much early twentieth-century discourse.

Angela's sense of liberty is continually circumscribed by her own restrictive classifications. And even though her passing rejects narrow categories for herself, she easily and unselfconsciously places taxonomic restrictions on others, paying a great deal of attention to social, ethnic, and national groups. In her effort to negotiate the urban community, however, she defines her colleagues through ethnic contrasts; this is evident, significantly, in her first art class. "She glanced around at the newcomers," Fauset writes of this first class, "a beautiful Jewess with pearly skin and a head positively foaming with curls, a tall Scandinavian, an obvious German, several more Americans" (95). Throughout the novel Angela sees very few Americans as "just Americans" (to use the phrase later coined by Jean Toomer), without qualifiers. John Banky, the most sympathetic of the newspaper reporters to whom she announced her "true racial identity," is described as "the young Hungarian" (352). Angela's attention to ethnic and racial categories, in fact, misrepresents these people. As a result, she misses the point: they are artists, journalists, intellectuals, and sociologists. Angela's belief that affecting whiteness will reconstitute her racial identity misunderstands the nature of identity itself. She embraces only one aspect of identity and overdetermines its significance. She participates, that is, in the same cultural predisposition to stereotype that her passing for white essentially seeks to dissolve. Lippmann explains the consequences: "Real space, real time, real numbers, real connections, real weights are lost. The perspective and the background and the dimensions of action are clipped and frozen in the stereotype" (*Opinion* 156).

Angela's elaborately constructed white identity is doomed to fail precisely because, like the racial distinctions it seeks to avoid, it depends on precisely the sort of arbitrary distinctions that her passing explicitly rejects. Her desire to maintain distinct personal spheres—to keep her romantic, professional, and artistic selves separate—predisposes her to catastrophe. In a brief but foreboding scene, Angela shirks Miss Powell's friendly approach for fear that Roger might witness their comradery. This rejection of Miss Powell reflects Angela's desire to keep Roger separate in her life from the small community of art students that constitutes her only circle of friends. Nor was it only Miss Powell whose familiarity she sought to hide from Roger—she separates him from all of her classmates, white and black: "she did not want any of the three, Martha, Paulette, nor Anthony to see whom she was meeting" (148). Miss Powell had, in fact, become part of a meaningful community for Angela; breaking out of her habitual reserve she had, on that day, hailed Angela, "pleased and excited. She laid her hand on Angela's arm but the latter shook her off" (149). These manipulations and elaborate orchestrations—maneuvering that anticipates Angela's furtive meeting with Jinny—reflect the impossibility of establishing a meaningful identity without first establishing meaningful connections. The flaws in Angela's means-to-ends reasoning become increasingly and painfully clear: she mistakenly views Roger's money as the end that will secure her happiness and believes that only dependence will yield independence. She fails to recognize that her love of art (and the company of others who share that love) is one way she can independently establish herself.

Angela's passing for white is doomed, too, because it demands that she separate herself from others on the arbitrary basis of race rather than on the organic basis of sympathy. In a chapter significantly titled "Search for the Great Community," John Dewey distinguishes between absolute freedom (the sort that demands Angela's elaborate manipulations and misrepresents her values) and meaningful liberty. Dewey's analysis summarizes the lesson of *Plum Bun*. "Liberty," he writes, "is that secure release and fulfillment of personal potentialities which take place only in rich and manifold association with others: the power to be an individualized self making a distinctive contribution and enjoying in its own way the fruits of association" (150). Even before Roger's ugly racism became evident, Angela realized that "there had been no touching point for their minds" (129). She admitted to Jinny, "I'm not in love with him at all"

(172). Yet in spite of the meaninglessness of her connection to Roger, she renounces the potentially rewarding intimacies of her classmates and ultimately rejects and endangers her sister to curry his favor.

The scene in which Angela abandons Jinny at the train station demonstrates the negative side of Angela's individualism and also illustrates the limits of Jinny's world. "I'm twenty three years old," Jinny thinks, "and I'm really all alone in the world" (167). Her embrace of family, tradition, and race has left her no better able to establish a meaningful identity than has Angela's rejection of those same values. Indeed, it aligns Jinny with Roger Fielding, who articulates a similar dissatisfaction and rootlessness. Jinny decides to sell the family home when the closed, self-contained, romanticized sphere of domestic fiction fails to sustain her as an adult. "There is such a shortage of houses in Philadelphia just now," she comments, "Mr. Hallowell says I can get at least twice as much as father paid for it" (169). Jinny changes when confronted with Angela's betrayal: "[s]omething hardened, grew cold within her" (167). And though Jinny becomes "almost swamped by friendships, pleasant intimacies, a thousand charming interests" in New York, she also becomes cunning. "I'm trying to look at things without sentiment" she tells Angela (241, 171).

One of the greatest ironies and most delicious oddities of *Plum Bun* is Angela's decision to announce her racial identity to a room full of newspaper reporters. Newspapers and art: the two cultural forces that finally frame Angela's ultimate establishment of a genuine and meaningful identity are forces that juxtapose language and image. But this development is hardly a narrative anomaly; indeed, the novel has fully anticipated that her denouement would be framed by such cultural features. Newspapers testify to the subsumption of distinctive communities by mass society. They illustrate the sheer vastness of life: what was once gossip and conversation is now commodified and mass marketed. By deciding to reveal her race to a group of reporters, Angela is, for the first time, using New York on her own terms, rather than being acted on or shaping her decisions to suit its demands. In this transition, her renunciation of whiteness affects the goal she sought by passing into it, as she discovers that the true meaning of freedom lies not in unequivocal liberty but in meaningful connection with others. As I have noted, white New York in the 1920s was much more interested in entertainment than in explicit political activity, but it is equally important to note that black New York believed that it could achieve political goals through artistic success;

Angela's experience draws together both of these dynamics and demonstrates their limits.

When Angela allows art to become the one constant and stable factor in her life, she finds her truest and best self. It structures her life economically: after Roger's rejection, she accepts a design job, and though the work "was a trifle narrow, a bit stultifying . . . it opened up possibilities" (235). Her attention to art gives her increasing purpose, precisely because it circumscribes a boundary of meaning within which she can establish her identity: "In the evenings she worked at the idea of a picture which she intended for a masterpiece. . . . But the urge to wander was no longer in the ascendent. The prospect of Europe did not seem as alluring now as the prospect of New York has appeared when she lived in Philadelphia. It would be nice to stay put, rooted; to have friends, experiences, memories" (240). When Angela structures her life's decisions around her artistic goals, her actions become more consistent with her values. Roger returns to propose marriage, and "she found herself hoping that he would not stay long. She wanted to think and she would like to paint" (317). Eventually, she realizes how strong the connection is between her art and her identity: "It both amused and saddened her to realize that her talent which she had once used as a blind to shield her real motives for breaking loose and coming to New York has now become the greatest, most real force in her life" (332). Angela's life is ordered by her art; in turn, her greatest work depicts "Life." Because Angela's art depends on images and not language, it affords her a means of expression free from the language of race but attentive to race's presence. Anthony cannot detect Mattie's race, for instance, based on Angela's sketch, but sees her instead as "a beautiful woman;—all woman" (282). Rather than generating a new self, painting permits Angela to uncover and enhance the self that already existed. By focusing on Angela's art as the key to her identity, *Plum Bun* celebrates an aspect of selfhood that is neither ignorant of race nor dependent on it.

At the novel's end, Angela explicitly articulates the novel's central assertion. "Yet when I begin to delve into it," she explains to Jinny, "the matter of blood seems nothing compared with individuality, character, living" (354). Indeed, Angela and Virginia both emerge at the novel's conclusion as women who have incorporated the best of both the black and the white worlds. Moreover, it is precisely because they ultimately define themselves wholly and individually, without regard for arbitrary or artificial barriers, that they establish such meaningful and successful identities in the end. As Angela departs for Europe, the circle of friends who surround her at the dock not only testify to the quality of her character, it also offers a model for a multiracial and genuinely multicultural society. Martha and Ladislas Starr, introduced specifically as "strong individualists" (113), are the liberal intellectual couple whose egalitarian marriage defies the expectations of their aristocratic families; they drive Angela to the dock. There, she is embraced by Ralph Ashley, who had earlier demonstrated his open-mindedness, saying "if I met a coloured woman of my own nationality, well-bred, beautiful, sympathetic, I wouldn't let the fact of her mixed blood stand in my way" (325). Mrs. Denver, "a wealthy woman from Butte, Montana" (249) appears at the dock as well. "'I couldn't stand seeing you go,' she said pitifully, 'without seeing you for one last time.' And, folding the girl in a close embrace, she broke down and murmured sadly of a lost daughter who would have been 'perhaps like you, dear, had she lived'" (371–72). Walter and Elizabeth Sandberg are there also, and the latter "clung to her, weeping" (372). This circle of friends who, as Ralph Ashley explains, all love Angela, represent a blend of generations, classes, ethnicities, political ideologies, and sympathies. They depict as well the complexion of a multidimensional, nuanced, and complex sense of self, for their friendship incorporates the universality of experience.

By the end, Fauset has offered ostensible closure—Angela has embraced her art, she has reunited with Jinny, and she has renounced marriage to Roger as a path to happiness. Yet though clear resolution is suggested, many of the novel's troubling complexities remain unresolved, and Fauset never renounces the implication that they are unresolvable. Anthony's arrival in Paris indicates that marriage will shape Angela's future. Angela's celebrated portrait of her mother is the work that defines her artistic development, yet this is a deracialized celebration of the woman who taught her to reject her sister. Similarly disconcerting is the fact that Angela declares her connection to Miss Powell by depriving her "sister" of those very things Miss Powell held so dear throughout the novel—her privacy and her dignity. And when Angela is finally reunited with Jinny, her sister tells her that she had known all along how much Angela was suffering in her lonely isolation. Jinny giggles at Angela's apology, admitting, "I'm a hard hearted little wretch. . . . I was just putting you through" (257). Jinny's admission offers a strategy for understanding

Fauset's intentions. It is a point worth noting, for instance, that the novel's closure depends on Angela's expatriation. Her multicultural circle of friends notwithstanding, Angela and Anthony are the only two individual characters who embody—literally—the contradictions of arbitrary racial classification. Has Fauset, in the end, been "putting Angela through"? Or, rather, is she putting *us* through, putting her culture through?

In delineating the limits of racial experience, Jessie Fauset reveals much about the racial dimensions of postwar modernism. Rather than maintaining a segregated fictional space where race circumscribes intellectual discourse, Fauset engages her world fully and directly, in a pointed and precise analysis of the racial dimensions of early twentieth-century American cultural anomie.

6 | Reading *Passing* through a Different Lens

Though critics regularly pair Jessie Fauset and Nella Larsen in a kind of literary racial sisterhood,[1] considerable evidence undermines the most earnest attempts to align them. It is true that they, along with Zora Neale Hurston, were the most prolific women novelists of the Harlem Renaissance, yet it is equally important to note that Fauset and Larsen moved in different social circles, they came from different backgrounds, and they maintained very different attitudes toward race. Their differences are perhaps most evident in a number of significant contrasts that can be drawn between Fauset's 1928 *Plum Bun* and Larsen's 1929 *Passing*, novels of passing that tend to be their most oft-cited works. These two novels not only illustrate and underscore the extent of their authors' biographical, literary, and philosophical differences, they provide strikingly parallel markers through which to examine the contrast. The year *Plum Bun* was published, for instance, Jessie Fauset married; in the year *Passing* was published, Nella Larsen contemplated divorce. *Plum Bun* employs tropes and narrative strategies evocative of nineteenth-century sentimental fiction, whereas the aesthetic sensibilities in *Passing* are decidedly modernist. In many other ways, both within the texts and without, *Passing* reverses *Plum Bun*'s most explicit claims about identity, community, and the role of race as a signifying category in the early twentieth century.

Passing contains no instance of biological or familial sisterhood; rather, it depicts the tense and duplicitous relationship between two women, Irene Redfield, a cultivated, privileged, light-skinned black woman and Clare Kendry, a childhood friend of Irene's who has spent her entire adult life passing for white. After the two are reunited, Clare

---

1. This is perhaps most explicitly articulated by Thadious M. Davis's biography of Larsen, who identifies Fauset as "one of [Larsen's] role models" (142) and asserts that she "saw in Fauset a reflection of the accomplished woman that she herself wanted, and intended to be" (143).

aggressively pursues Irene's friendship, partly from a sense of personal nostalgia and partly because she feels increasingly consumed by her desire to reconnect with "her people." Because Irene lives in Harlem and interacts regularly with fashionable black society, Clare uses her friendship with Irene to reenter black society, though she does so behind the back of her racist white husband. Irene resists and resents Clare's presence in her life and in black culture, in part because Clare's beauty, glamour, and innate vivacity arouse both jealousy (Irene thinks that Clare is having an affair with her husband Brian) and desire (Irene cannot resist her own sexually charged attraction to Clare). In the novel's denouement, Clare's husband discovers her "true" racial identity and rushes into a Harlem party to confront her. When he enters, Irene runs to Clare, who has been sitting at an open window in the seventeenth-floor apartment, and Clare falls (or is pushed by Irene) to her death.

As has been noted, the critical predisposition to view Nella Larsen and Jessie Fauset as racial sisters forms the basis of many literary analyses of the two writers in general and of their two passing novels in particular. Yet if we shift our lens and alter the focus, several striking narrative parallels indicate an ideological disconnect between the passing of Fauset's and Larsen's protagonists, underscoring the contrapositions of the two novels. As *Plum Bun* ends, Angela Murray leaves New York for Europe; yet as *Passing* begins, Clare Kendry has just returned from Europe, longing for Harlem. In *Plum Bun*, Angela regains Jinny's sisterly affection, whereas in *Passing*, Clare incites Irene to a sort of sibling rivalry (another reason to view with suspicion critical attempts to align the two writers as sisters[2]). Oppositions of plot affect each novel's leading male character as well: in *Plum Bun* Anthony claims Brazilian heritage, but his mother has left her country behind to adopt U.S. citizenship; whereas in *Passing* Brian Redfield, Irene's husband, despises the United States and longs to live in South America. Likewise, though Fauset employs the "Plum Bun" nursery rhyme, complete with a moral that, as Deborah McDowell argues, provides an ironic contrast to the realities of race and gender,[3] Larsen

---

2. Helena Michie's reading of the novel, in her aptly titled *Sororophobia*, underscores the rivalry between them and shrewdly notes that the very word *sister* contains political implications that evoke "a fantasy version of black sisterhood" (137).

3. For McDowell, the choice of epigraph "focuses on the powerful role fairy tales play in conditioning women to idealize marriage and romantic love as the source of their completeness as well as their marital well-being" (*Changing* 66).

cites the ambiguously enumerative, "Rich man, poor man, / Beggar man, thief, / Doctor, lawyer, / Indian chief." Cinderella references in the narrative of *Passing* depict Clare Kendry as "the blonde beauty out of the fairy tale," yet her ending proves far more tragic than that of Angela Murray. These sharp contrasts indicate how definitively the narrative of *Passing* repudiates that of *Plum Bun,* for as Fauset focuses explicitly on Angela's attempts to pass from black to white, Larsen examines Clare Kendry's return from white to black. Such opposition underscores the ideological dissimilarity of the two novels, simultaneously revealing the stretch required to view Fauset and Larsen as "sisters." Indeed, Larsen's novel reveals homicidal tendencies in the figure most evocative of Fauset herself. Whether we read Irene's complicity in Clare's death as deliberate or psychological, the fact remains that Larsen's satire kills off the free-spirited individualist and preserves the prim, race-conscious, social doyenne.

Larsen does align *Passing* repeatedly and specifically with another Harlem Renaissance novel, however, but one written by a white man: Carl Van Vechten's controversial, best-selling 1926 *Nigger Heaven.* Though Larsen's references to Van Vechten's work are often briefly noted, they have never been fully explored or seriously analyzed—a significant, resonant, and multifaceted omission in my estimation. Indeed, Pamela Caughie's nuanced analysis *Passing and Pedagogy* begins by noting that a remark made in passing often opens up unexpected, uncontrollable, and multifaceted revelations about a speaker. "A passing comment," she notes, "is too often seen *only* as a slip of the mask, revealing the true character behind the persona" (1). Caughie's argument finds the sites of conflict revealed by such offhanded remarks to be "anything but incidental," and the truth of this observation is clearly evident here. To examine the connections between *Passing* and *Nigger Heaven* requires that we shift our lens and focus once again: in so doing, we see the depth and substance of Larsen's relationship with Carl Van Vechten; we confront her novel's emphatic rebellion against the racial politics that influenced Harlem's artists and writers; and we engage Larsen's bitter critique of the social codes promoted in the fiction of Jessie Fauset. Indeed, the novel of passing that emerges when reading through such a lens is one that demonstrates Larsen's outright hostility toward genteel black womanhood, the very identity that *Passing* is generally held to value and the sort that Fauset's novels ostensibly embrace.

When Carl Van Vechten published *Nigger Heaven,* he offended, shocked, delighted, and amused his readers in equal measure. Though the scandalous title brought perhaps the strongest and swiftest response, the novel itself offers a multifaceted meditation on racial authenticity. *Nigger Heaven* continually undermines any effort to categorize race: the poles of reason and emotion, rich and poor, cultured and crude, primitive and civilized simply do not apply in the Harlem of *Nigger Heaven.* The controversy caused by Van Vechten's novel brought unprecedented attention to Harlem's social and artistic culture and created a market for African American literature. *Nigger Heaven* also provided an occasion for intellectuals—black and white—to debate black America's literary potential as well as its artistic representation. *The Crisis,* the literary journal of the NAACP, was already examining this question in detail in a serialized symposium, "The Negro in Art: How Shall He Be Portrayed?" Responses from a range of sympathetic whites and blacks illustrated, perhaps for the first time, the complexity of issues such as racial authenticity and literary representation. "When the artist, white or black, portrays Negro characters," asks the symposium's first question, "is he under any obligation or limitations as to the sort of character he will portray?" The second question presses on, "Can any author be criticized for painting the worst or the best characters of a group?" The journal's literary editor, Jessie Fauset, and the NAACP's cofounder, W. E. B. Du Bois, privately agreed that the white reading public's increasing interest in younger writers like Langston Hughes and Rudolph Fisher had emerged from a prurient fascination with primitivism, and the survey intended to support this belief and to critique its implications. These questions raise the very issues for which *Nigger Heaven* was most harshly attacked. Like many readers of the *Crisis* symposium in 1926, however, many critics of today are unaware that, in fact, Carl Van Vechten was ghostwriter of the questions that constitute the symposium. This is, I believe, an important and telling irony, and a fact of which Nella Larsen may well have been aware.[4]

Though Van Vechten's response to the *Crisis* symposium was published six months before *Nigger Heaven*—it was composed during the

---

4. See Emily Bernard's introduction to *Remember Me to Harlem,* xix. Van Vechten's biographer, Bruce Kellner, confirms his authorship based not only on interviews with Van Vechten himself but also from the typescripts in Van Vechten's papers, in his distinctive typewriting, at Yale (Bruce Kellner, e-mail to the author, 12 Oct. 1999).

same week he wrote the most controversial cabaret scenes for *Nigger Heaven*—it indicates his self-consciousness of the fine line he walks in writing the novel. He sympathizes with those who, like Fauset and Du Bois, are sensitive to negative portrayals of the race ("heaven knows," he wrote, "he has reason enough to feel sensitive") but argues that such an attitude is "completely inimical to art." He laments the self-censorship among black writers that causes them "to refrain from using valuable material," and cites Rudolph Fisher as a rare exception. Van Vechten ominously notes that if "a white man had written [such stories] he would be called a Negro hater," an observation that proved portentous when W. E. B. Du Bois later accused *Nigger Heaven* of having "not a single loveable character" ("Critiques" 107). Like the white writers portrayed in *Nigger Heaven*, Van Vechten celebrates the "wealth of novel, exotic, picturesque material" to be found in both the "squalor" and the "vice" of "Negro life." His essay's closing question resonates: "Are Negro writers going to write about this exquisite material while it is still fresh or will they continue to make a free gift of it to white authors who will exploit it until not a drop of vitality remains?"

The tension over so-called true racial identity, evident in the theme of passing, also plays out in the debate over *Nigger Heaven* and, indeed, is richly manifested in the figure of Van Vechten himself. Nella Larsen's *Passing* participates in this debate; it presents a thinly veiled response to W. E. B. Du Bois's harsh review of Van Vechten and his novel. The characters, plot, conclusions, and subtexts that emerge in *Passing* engage Du Bois's own empowering metaphor from *The Souls of Black Folk* by demonstrating that genuine "soul" is colorless and can, in fact, abide in an apparently white body. To be sure, Clare brings "a touching gladness that welled up and overflowed" and "talk and merriment" to Harlem when she visits. The sympathy that Larsen builds for Clare in *Passing*, and the narrative sensibility that celebrates Clare's deep sympathy for black culture and her passionate desire to connect with it specifically implicate Van Vechten. This heretofore unnoted subtext both challenges and belies the categorizing tendencies of critics who read the novel solely—and perhaps reductively—in terms of other black women writers' work.

Du Bois's bitter and angry review has been cited often and has informed much of the criticism directed toward *Nigger Heaven*, then and now. By equivocating author and novel, Du Bois invoked an ideology of racial authenticity in which Van Vechten was cast as a racial interloper, one who offers "an affront to the hospitality of black folk and to the intelligence of white" (106). The review's thesis revolves around an implicit assumption that racial identity mediates aesthetic experience. "Van Vechten has never heard a sob in a cabaret," he charges. "All he hears is noise and brawling" (107). By way of (explicitly racialized) contrast, Du Bois cites Langston Hughes's poetry as the better alternative, for Hughes "whispers." In *Passing*, Larsen offers a response to the Du Boisian school of racialist thought, a critique of what is now termed "identity politics" that pointed specifically—and affirmatively—to Van Vechten's right to write *Nigger Heaven*. Du Bois's review dismisses the conclusion of *Nigger Heaven*, charging, "The final climax is an utterly senseless murder which appears without preparation or reason from the clouds" (108). Larsen responds in *Passing* by contriving an ending that literalizes Du Bois's metaphor—Clare's death does, indeed, fall from the clouds.

From its first pages, Larsen's novel explicitly evokes Van Vechten's famous "Negro novel": *Passing* cites the same Countee Cullen poem, "Heritage," that serves as the epigraph to *Nigger Heaven*. And Larsen signals the connectedness of these citations in her choice of lines, as she cites—as did Carl Van Vechten—only from the poem's few italicized sections. Van Vechten's epigraph for *Nigger Heaven* features the opening sentence of Cullen's italicized final stanza, a politically resonant line that refers to the poet's place in a racially contentious society: *"All day long and all night through, / One thing only must I do: / Quench my pride and cool my blood, / Lest I perish in the flood."* Larsen's epigraph for *Passing* highlights the poem's first italicized lines, an evocative query that articulates the narrator's sense of alienation from his ancestors: *"One three centuries removed / From the scenes his fathers loved, / Spicy grove, cinnamon tree, / What is Africa to me?"* Larsen's page of acknowledgments again underscores the works' parallels: Van Vechten dedicates his novel to his wife Fania Marinoff, and Larsen dedicates hers to Van Vechten and Marinoff both. Beth McCoy's excellent analysis of the typographical similarities between *Passing* and *Nigger Heaven* details the visual similarities between the two books. "Both books were set in Caslon, and thus both books look similarly authoritative and contemporaneous," she explains. "As a Knopf text set in Caslon, Larsen's novel looks like neither a subordinate nor a supplicant to Van Vechten's" (109).

Nella Larsen structures *Passing* by using a narrative strategy evocative of the architecture of Van Vechten's novel, ordering it into three sections

(Encounter, Re-Encounter, Finale) that offer transitions and closure similar to those in *Nigger Heaven* (Prologue, Book One, Book Two). Comparable trajectories of plot enhance the effect: the action of *Passing* begins as Irene rides an elevator up into a cool rooftop escape from the sweltering crowds and Chicago's unforgiving heat and ends with Clare's brutal fall from a penthouse window into the snow of a winter night; *Nigger Heaven*'s bracketing scenes, those for which, as Larsen well knew, Van Vechten was most harshly criticized for "noise and brawling," are scenes of descent into the underground of raunchy, gin-soaked cabaret life. Both novels end with a death and the subsequent appearance of a police officer: in Van Vechten's, "a coat of blue buttoned with brass" (284) and in Larsen's "a strange man, authoritative and official" (114). This close association connects the very scenes of *Nigger Heaven* that caused the greatest conflict and turmoil for Van Vechten with those in *Passing* that reveal both the hypocrisy of Harlem's racial politics and its cost, namely Irene's occasional passing and Clare's death.

The working title for *Passing* was "Nig," an explicit reference to Van Vechten's work, and the strength of Larsen's identification with the man and his novel cannot be overstated. She regularly updated him about her work on the novel and conceived of it, even in the planning stages, as a tribute to him. In a letter to Van Vechten on 7, March 1927, Larsen writes of her relief at having completed *Quicksand,* her first novel: "Heaven forbid that I should ever be bitten by the desire to write another novel! Except, perhaps, one to dedicate to you. For, why should Langston Hughes be the only one to enjoy notoriety for the sake of his convictions?" As Emily Bernard explains, this banter, which refers to Hughes's having dedicated his 1927 *Fine Clothes to the Jew* to Van Vechten, reveals much about the publishing industry's racial attitudes. "Hughes's 'conviction,'" Bernard notes, "was a determination to publish what he wished despite the opinions of critics, black or white" ("Black" 117). Such self-protective disregard served Hughes well, too, as the response to both the blues and jazz idiom of his poetry and the ostensibly anti-Semitic title (which derives from the poem "Hard Luck" in the lines, "When hard luck overtakes you / Nothin' for you to do / Gather up yo' fine clothes / An' sell 'em to de Jew") was fast, furious, and personal. Arnold Rampersad summarized the response to Hughes's poetry as one in which, according to his critics, in "pandering to the taste of whites for the sensational . . . Hughes had betrayed his race" (141). When Nella Larsen aligns herself with Carl Van

Vechten and Langston Hughes, specifically in relation to their most controversial works, she reveals her desire for the intimacy with Van Vechten that Hughes clearly claims, and she more emphatically seeks the sort of publicity that their two books garnered. In her correspondence, as in her fiction, Larsen reveals her willingness to tease racial presumptions and identify racial hypocrisy in much the same way that Van Vechten and Hughes do.

On completing the manuscript that would become *Passing*, Larsen wrote to tell Van Vechten that she had finished "[his] novel." Though she ultimately changed the title from the deliberately provocative "Nig" to the more neutral "Passing," the moniker "Nig," in Larsen's work, refers specifically to Clare Kendry, and *her* connection to Van Vechten warrants consideration, for in the racial landscape of Larsen's fictional world, as in 1920s Harlem itself, both Van Vechten and Clare are cast as interlopers. Though Cheryl Wall reads Clare's name as an ironic contrast to her "opaque character" (122), one need only place the names Clare and Carl alongside each other to see their dramatic rhetorical similarity.[5] Moreover, anyone who has read through Van Vechten's correspondence and notebooks will recognize that the description of Clare's handwriting—its purple ink, its unusual paper size, its foreign demeanor, its "almost illegible scrawl"—also describes Van Vechten's favored writing implements and penmanship. Larsen's attention to Clare's "catlike" nature surely had special resonance for her dear friend and mentor, who was himself devoted to cats (a fact commemorated in his personal bookplate), having written a popular book in tribute to *The Tiger in the House*. Carl Van Vechten, Harlem's ever-present "honorary Negro," once described himself as "violently addicted to Negroes" in summarizing his attraction to Harlem. "But it soon became obvious to me," Van Vechten later recalled, "that I would write about these people because my feeling about them was very strong" (Typescript 197). Emily Bernard has shrewdly noted that the similarity between Van Vechten's "addiction" and Clare's passion for black Harlem also makes it difficult to sustain any meaningful connection between Van Vechten and Hugh Wentworth, the white writer in *Passing* who is often taken for his putative fictional counterpart. In contrast to Wentworth's aloof withdrawal, Clare's enthusiasm, like Van Vechten's, is hyperbolic: "I am *so* excited," Clare cries on the way to the

---

5. My thanks to Bruce Kellner for pointing this out.

NWA dance. "You can't possibly imagine! It's marvellous to be really on the way! I can hardly believe it!!" (74). Hugh Wentworth's surfaces may align him with Van Vechten, but little else substantiates the connection.

Indeed, critics who easily accept and quickly dispense with the ostensible parallels between Van Vechten and Wentworth tend to ignore or dismiss the more resonant differences between the two. Irene Redfield wears a "tiny triumphant smile" in announcing her friendship with Hugh Wentworth, and the novel makes it clear that they are close. But as a stand-in for Carl Van Vechten, Hugh Wentworth not only falls short, he also lacks the very qualities that made Van Vechten "dangerous" (like Clare) and that would have absolutely repelled someone like Irene Redfield. By his own testimony, Van Vechten spent a good portion of the late 1920s drunk: he partied much, slept little, cultivated homosexual liaisons, encouraged writers, listened to blues and jazz, and sought the acquaintance and friendship of black folk of all social strata. He was hardly the sort of person who would appeal to Irene Redfield, a woman who gives fastidious tea parties, who sleeps often, who cannot utter the word *sex*, who destroys Clare's letter and disregards her appeals for friendship, whose first gesture in the novel is to escape the masses of sweltering bodies, and who entertains no familiarity with her servants. In arguing that Hugh provides a "screen" for the exploration of Irene's thoughts, Emily Bernard succinctly summarizes his primary function, wisely observing that "Hugh Wentworth exists mainly for Irene's purposes" ("Black" 145). But it is important to note that his function as a screen contains no meaningful connection to Carl Van Vechten. Clare dislikes Hugh Wentworth's writing because it is "contemptuous. . . . As if he more or less despised everything and everybody" (69). Yet in one of her earliest letters to Carl Van Vechten, Nella Larsen praises him for *not* demonstrating this very characteristic: "It is nice to find someone writing as if he didn't absolutely despise the age in which he lives,"[6] she writes, her admiration for Van Vechten a stark contrast to her characterization of Hugh Wentworth.

---

6. (11 Aug. 1925) This line precedes the oft-quoted passage that forms the epigraph to Thadious Davis's biography of Larsen: "And surely it is more interesting to belong to one's own time, to share its peculiar vision, catch the flying glimpse of the panorama which no subsequent generation can ever recover." That Davis neglects to identify the letter's recipient and fails to include its opening compliment says much about the critical response to the friendship and critical exchange about Larsen and Van Vechten.

Discarding the facile and misleading association between Van Vechten and Hugh Wentworth reveals Larsen's novel to be a sly and fascinating critique of Harlem's racial politics, one that, significantly, links its depiction of hypocritical self-delusion along an axis connecting Clare and her moniker "Nig," Van Vechten and his novel *Nigger Heaven*. Clare's passing for white thus evokes Van Vechten's own ability to pass across an ideological color line. The historical problem with Van Vechten, the man dubbed by Zora Neale Hurston to be Harlem's "Negrotarian," was very much like the fictional problem with Clare, because both, as "honorary Negroes," offer a model of passing for black. In explaining her fondness for Van Vechten, Hurston once said, "If Carl was a people instead of a person, I could then say, these are my people" (Watson 100), her comment exposing the permeability of coherent racial categories. Zora Neale Hurston was but one of many of Van Vechten's friends, colleagues, and critics who commented specifically on his uncanny success at passing for black, his ability to effect "racechanges," to use Susan Gubar's term. Several caricatures of Van Vechten by artist Miguel Covarrubias underscore this point, as they present images that, as Gubar explains, "Capture not so much Van Vechten in blackface as Van Vechten the African American" (154). One of the more distinctly black renderings is suggestively titled "A Prediction." Likewise, the playwright Avery Hopwood referred to Van Vechten as his "black and white buddy" and wrote humorously to his friend, on reading *Nigger Heaven,* about the author's racial sympathies:

> Of course, everyone is bound to ask how you acquired such an intimate knowledge of Harlem, and to say, "Why, he must have lived there!" I am explaining to them, however, that that is not the case—that you really see little of Harlem, these days, but that you saw a great deal of it before you *passed*. They are all so surprised to hear about your negro strain, but I tell them that your best friends *always knew*. . . . And no matter how other people treat you, I shall remain the same.
>
> I also explained that you are The Abraham Lincoln of the Colored Race. But Oh, Carl, my Carlo, have you ever stopped to consider *what happened to Lincoln?*

All who knew Van Vechten knew about his intense involvement in and fondness for black culture. His emotional connection and sympathetic identification is perhaps most explicit in a letter to Langston Hughes in which he notes, "you and I are the only colored people who really love *niggers*." (Rampersad 145; 25, March 1927).

When, in Nella Larsen's novel, Irene tells Hugh, "It's easy for a Negro to 'pass' for white. But I don't think it would be so simple for a white person to 'pass' for colored" (78), she does not echo Larsen's feelings about Carl Van Vechten. "Was it you or another who told me of the shocked horror of one of your friends because 'Carl Van Vechten knows a Negro?'" Larsen wrote to him in praise of *Nigger Heaven,*

> Well! What will she say when she reads this shy story, with its air of decep-
> tive simplicity and discovers that Carl Van Vechten knows the Negro?
>
> It is a fine tale, this story of the deterioration and subsequent ruin of a
> weakling who blames all his troubles on that old scapegoat, the race prob-
> lem. Dangerous too. But with what exquisite balance you have avoided the
> propagandistic pitfall. But of course, *you* would. Like your Lasca Sartoris,
> who so superbly breasts the flood of racial prejudices (black and white . . .).
> You see its too close, too true, as if you had undressed the lot of us and
> turned on a strong light too. I feel a kind of despair. Why, oh, why, couldn't
> we have done something as big as this for ourselves? Fear, I suppose. It is big,
> big in its pity, big in its cruelties. (11 Aug. 1926)

The idea that Van Vechten had "undressed the lot of us" further distances Larsen's sensibilities from those of Irene, as it seems to contradict Irene's sense that passing for black proves more difficult than passing for white. To the contrary, the sexually suggestive language implies Van Vechten's genuine intimacy with the race and draws attention to the aura of sexual intrigue that always surrounded him. Indeed, the provocative and important argument presented by Deborah McDowell and developed by Ann duCille about the lesbian subtext that animates *Passing* contains a fascinating counterpart in Carl Van Vechten's own openly homosexual activity and in what Jonathan Weinberg has termed his "queer collection" of gay pornography and homoerotic photography of both black and white men. To consider the implications of this intersection of racial and sexual indeterminacy is to understand the resonance of Pamela Caughie's assertion that "passing is the site where the often competing narratives of racial and gender oppression converge on the issue of sexuality" (193).

Aligning Clare with Carl, Larsen aligns her book with Van Vechten's, and this complex association transforms the passing character into a vehicle for social analysis. That Clare's return to the black community is conspicuously framed in references to language and writing suggests the interconnectedness of race, writing, and selfhood, and the specificity of her purple ink (to recall just one of the aforementioned references) makes the intersection historically and personally specific. Sandra Gilbert and Susan Gubar observe that the novel opens with a letter and propose that by aligning writing and passing, "the novel's emphasis on writing and specifically on letter-writing extends Larsen's psychological study of inauthenticity to examine an aesthetic issue" (153). And indeed, this is true: writing, like passing, is an act of self-generation; both are independently and willfully creative acts. More to the point, Clare's *racial* passing ends at the cost of her life's passing, in the sense that *passing* also operates as the primary euphemism for death. In such an ending, we see the interconnectedness between the many meanings of *passing,* and Larsen draws our attention to the multivalent nature and manipulability of language.

Significantly, Clare's writing precedes and predicts her presence in the novel. Her letter demands interpretation and encodes marks of difference into its material presence. Clare's alienation from Irene's social world is inscribed on the envelope, which seems, when compared to Irene's "other and clearly directed letters . . . out of place and alien" (9). Before reading the letter's *words* as its text, however, Irene reads its *appearance* for its import, extrapolating meaning from the way it looks. She notices its "[p]urple ink" and "[f]oreign paper of extraordinary size" and thereby characterizes it as "mysterious and slightly furtive" and a "thin sly thing" (9). The letter's outward appearance simultaneously alludes to its "purple" prose: "For I am lonely, so lonely," Clare has written, "[I] cannot help longing to be with you, as I have never longed for anything before" (11). Critics have commented on the significance of the letter's appearance as well: Claudia Tate, for instance, argues that "the letter resembles the extraordinary physical appearance of Clare Kendry" ("Nella" 144). This emphasis on appearance as an indicator of true racial identity has been proved repeatedly unreliable in the novel, however. The premise and the hope of passing is exactly the opposite—that appearance can misrepresent.

Letters between Clare and Irene carry tremendous symbolic weight in *Passing.* The two letters that Clare writes to Irene frame the novel's opening "Encounter" section. Central to understanding their symbolic import is the fact that Clare's last letter appears first, and her first letter last. Reconsidering that first note—one that Irene "had instinctively known came from Clare Kendry, though she couldn't remember ever having had a letter from her before" (46)—one recognizes how literally Clare's self, her body, is connected to written text. Irene's fear of and anger toward Clare causes her to destroy the note: "With unusual methodicalness she tore the offending letter into tiny ragged squares that fluttered down and made a small heap in her black *crepe de Chine* lap. The destruction completed, she gathered them up, rose, and moved to the train's end. Standing there, she dropped them over the railing and watched them scatter, on tracks, on cinder, on forlorn grass, in rills of dirty water" (47). Here, then, is a gesture foretelling Clare's death. For at the novel's conclusion, Clare drops out the apartment window, leaving, as Irene imagines it, "her glorious body mutilated" (113) on the ground, just as her words are dismantled and scattered early on. The novel's conclusion thus reconciles Clare's written self with her corporeal self, as both are mutilated and discarded. The image of Clare's body landing in "the white ground below" (110), already known to be "lovely with that undisturbed snow" (109), is never explicitly invoked after she falls, though careful descriptions have prepared us to imagine such a site.[7]

Whether intentional or not (and the specificity of Nella Larsen's references to florid penmanship and purple ink clearly indicate some degree of intentionality), the letters that frame *Passing* necessarily point to the letters that frame Larsen's personal friendship with Van Vechten. Yet whereas Clare's letters long for connection with Harlem's black community, Larsen's letters often critique Harlem's hypocrisy and resist its ap-

---

7. Nella Larsen herself later re-created and thereby exploited this symbolic moment, further underscoring that the tangled connections between fiction and life were created, in this instance with great drama and flair, by Larsen. In the early 1930s, she traveled to Nashville to join her husband Dr. Elmer Imes, then a professor of physics at Fisk University. Their marriage had long been unstable, Imes having fallen deeply in love with Ethel Gilbert, a white Fisk administrator, but also having declared and demonstrated his intention to "do right" by Nella (providing continual financial support, for instance). Thadious Davis details the culture of gossip that brought Larsen to the campus and that her arrival failed to assuage. "One rumor was so widespread and persistent," Davis notes, "that it appeared in the headlines of a national African-American newspaper: 'Recall "Jump" From Window.' Reportedly, Larsen had 'jumped or had fallen out of a window and done herself bodily harm" (407). Clearly, she intended for these erratic actions to evoke Clare Kendry's death.

peals to racial solidarity. One of the most pointed examples of this mind-set comes in a letter Larsen wrote to Dorothy Peterson, in which she refers to her novel *Quicksand* in explaining her desire to move to a new apartment. "Right now when I look out into the Harlem streets," Larsen writes, "I feel just like Helga Crane in my novel. Furious at being con-nected with all these niggers." Larsen regularly used colloquial refer-ences to race when writing to Van Vechten as well, referring to blacks as *shines* or *niggers* in a manner that continually suggests not only the racial intimacy between the two but also a shared skepticism about race loyalty. "I should love to have seen the reviews in the nigger papers," she writes to him of George Schuyler's *Black No More.* "Dorothy sent me two from the ofays" (3 March 1931). Occasionally, the letters hint at a provocative but undisclosed dimension to their relationship. "Almost I had a fit of nervous prostration," she wrote on 6 April 1927, "Because in the move I thought I had lost your letters—and that possibly Elmer [her husband] had found them."

The opening pages of *Passing* thus direct us to Carl Van Vechten and *Nigger Heaven* and to the broader implications raised by such a parallel. For just as the novel relates Clare's writing to her character, it also reveals the complexities that result from Irene's willingness to read her world like a text (a highly romanticized misreading, as I later show) and thereby calls attention to the relationship between texts and characters, between writing and selfhood. In detailing the parallels between "the double logic of writing" and the "logic of passing"—both strategies for simultaneously concealing and revealing the self—Pamela Caughie shrewdly reminds us that "writing never delivers the control it promises, for we still expose ourselves in ways we had not intended or realized" (3). Irene's inability to control her world thus stems from her misreading of it.

As an "honorary Negro," Carl Van Vechten acquired local fame, evi-dent in the frequency with which his parties were reported in Harlem newspaper society pages and later in the 1930 lyrics of Andy Razaf's "Go Harlem," which encouraged visits to Harlem, "Like Van Vechten, Start in-spectin'." Likewise, passing for white permits Clare to transform herself into a meaningful social presence, as her white skin claims a higher mar-ket value than her black blood; she knows that a beautiful white woman is more marriageable than a beautiful black one. Significantly, Clare's passing—her self-production—acquires commercial value and her iden-tity acquires social agency in direct relation to Nella Larsen's literary productivity. For Clare cashes in on the considerable market value of her physical body, just as writing the novel *Passing* promised to legitimate Nella Larsen's claim to established authorship. Larsen articulated her own desire to make money with crass specificity in one letter to Carl Van Vechten; she writes, "There is a new Negro magazine . . . to which I have been asked to contribute, but since money is my ultimate goal, I am afraid I won't be able to do it" (5 Oct. 1928). One can clearly identify the connection to Carl Van Vechten in this intersection of passing and writing: *Nigger Heaven* was his only "Negro novel" and his only best-seller, far more profitable than any of his other books. That Van Vechten understood the market value of blackness is manifestly clear in his response to the 1926 symposium, "The Negro in Art: How Should He Be Portrayed?" in *The Crisis*. Recall that his essay's closing question resonates with market logic: "Are Negro writers going to write about this exquisite material while it is still fresh or will they continue to make a free gift of it to white authors who will exploit it until not a drop of vitality remains?"

Clare's return to her black identity takes place in a Harlem where Irene's elitist class distinctions challenge the role of race in defining communities. For as much as Clare Kendry embodies the sort of radical individualism made manifest by the white Van Vechten's notorious "inspectin'," Irene Redfield is a creature of her community in precisely the ways that Du Bois promoted. Nella Larsen was often cattily critical of the presumptuousness that sometimes surrounded Du Bois, and it is small wonder that Irene's character becomes Larsen's sounding board. In one instance, Larsen received solicitation for a $100 donation toward Du Bois's birthday present, a $2500 gift. "Some nerve I say," she wrote Van Vechten. "I'm about to celebrate a birthday too and I feel like writing and telling them that. I could use $2500 myself. In fact I think it will do me more good at thirty five than him at sixty" (19 Mar. 1928). She similarly betrayed her biting cynicism about pretentious affairs, particularly those associated with NAACP social events, and often described them as "dicty," using the popular Harlem slang word to describe the swells of the so-called talented tenth. When the NAACP Women's Auxiliary planned a tea in her honor, her conditional enthusiasm revealed a suspicious hostility. "The good God only knows why," she wrote to Van Vechten. "I hope you will get an invitation because this will be a time when I will need all of my friends" (1 May 1928).

Much of Nella Larsen's personal resentment for such "dicty" presumptions reveals itself in Irene Redfield, the most self-consciously and avowedly race-conscious character in the novel. Indeed, Irene's exaggerated gentility, her attention to social propriety, her desire for safety in the service of race loyalty satirizes the Du Boisian idea of "soul"—blackness as an internalized and constant identity—and casts it cynically as something external and wholly manipulable, more a fashion statement than an ideology. Irene Redfield's narrow, selfish character derives from an avowed adherence to race and a genuine concern for class; her refusal or inability to recognize and acknowledge her motives provides the most damning commentary of Harlem's racial politics. Larsen's disgust for hypocrisy such as that demonstrated by Irene when she maintains an aloof distance from her dark-skinned servants is everywhere evident in her personal correspondence. For instance, she advised Van Vechten, "About the Spingarn Medal. If you got it, you'd be lynched—by Negroes. Take my advice, refuse it, 'graciously but firmly'" (6 Oct. 1926).

Irene Redfield's characterization as a frigid, supercilious, self-deluded prig thus shatters the myth of moral superiority of blacks promoted by Du Bois and Jessie Fauset. George Hutchinson has noted that "many of Fauset's attributes match those of women Larsen attacks in her fiction" ("Nella" 343), and this point is also evident repeatedly in Larsen's personal correspondence. Indeed, her letters to Van Vechten throughout 1926 indicate that the two shared a skeptical attitude about the prevailing racial politics in Harlem and elsewhere. One letter begins by disparaging her husband's family. "It was nice to have your letter yesterday when I got back from tiresome visit in Philadelphia among the ultra religious," she writes. "Have you noticed that when Nordics talk against the admission of Negroes to their homes, etc., it is rank prejudice [sic], but when we take the same attitude about white folks it is race loyalty?" (12 Nov. 1926). Irene's response to Clare fictionally illustrates the pettiness of the color-consciousness within the black community that Larsen critiques in her letters to Van Vechten. Moreover, Irene's obsessive need to maintain order suggests the brittle, tenuous nature of the boundaries she seeks to maintain.

Certainly, the relationship between class affiliation and selfhood are singularly important to Irene. Feeling herself under Clare's scrutiny at the tearoom of the Drayton Hotel, Irene initially worries not about racial detection but rather that she has unwittingly committed a social or fashion faux pas. She feels "guardedly" to be sure that she had not "put her hat on backwards." She considers the possibility of "a streak of powder somewhere on her face," and she checks to be certain that there is not "something wrong with her dress" (149). Only after she has assured herself that her appearance bespeaks a cultivated, feminine, and polished demeanor does Irene worry that her blackness is somehow interpretable. "Did that woman," she then wonders, "could that woman somehow know that here before her very eyes on the roof of the Drayton sat a Negro?" (150). Irene worries less, that is, that her apparent whiteness might misrepresent her actual blackness than that her apparent sloppiness might misrepresent her actual gentility.

Such scenes reveal the self-deception through which Irene filters all of her thoughts about race. In a moment of agonizing self-pity, she cites race as the primary restriction in her life and attributes her desire for tranquility and security to her need to countermand racial suffering: "She was caught between two allegiances, different, yet the same. Herself. Her race. Race! The thing that bound and suffocated her. Whatever steps she took, or if she took none at all, something would be crushed. . . . It was, she cried silently, enough to suffer as a woman, an individual, on one's own account without having to suffer for the race as well" (225). Yet as Cheryl Wall has shrewdly observed, Irene is apparently unmoved by any sense of racial injustice in the face of Jack Bellew's obnoxious screed. "Irene is certain that she alone takes offense at Bellew's racist vitriol," Wall notes, "but when they leave, it is Gertrude [who] expresses outrage. Irene imagines, by contrast, that 'under other conditions,' she could like Jack Bellew" (126–27). Clare Kendry thus challenges the coherence and order in Irene's Harlem, and her vibrant presence reveals Irene to be merely aristocratic and fastidious. Irene embraces such class-bound behavior and values because she hopes they will stabilize and contain her world. Instead, her world seems to be everywhere escaping her control: "Yet all the while, in spite of her searchings and feeling of frustration, she was aware that, to her, security was the most important and desired thing in life. . . . She wanted only to be tranquil" (235). She not only interprets tranquility through her willed ignorance—she also mistakes that ignorance for tranquility.

Newspapers threaten and intimidate Irene's race-conscious propriety in much the same way that *Nigger Heaven* outraged Du Bois. His energetic denunciation has been quoted often, and it is forceful and clear. "Real human feelings are laughed at. Love is degraded," Du Bois writes of Van

Vechten's novel. "Life to him is just one damned orgy after another, with hate, hurt, gin and sadism" ("Critiques" 107). With similar impatience, Irene is unreasonably annoyed when Brian conspicuously reads a newspaper at breakfast, picking it up with "his long, nervous fingers" and making "a little rattling noise" very much like the "audible crunching sound that Irene disliked so intensely" (185). She recoils against knowledge of the outside world because her own small social world cannot account for its challenges to her sense of racial identity. In Finale, then, when "Brian spoke bitterly of a lynching that he had been reading about in the evening paper. . . . Irene's voice was a plea and a rebuke" (102).

In contrast to the newspaper reports Irene shuns, she romanticizes her own experiences by using literary language that, at best, obfuscates reality. When Irene invokes the "Rich man, poor man" nursery rhyme to describe her impressions of the NWA dance to Hugh Wentworth at the end of the novel, she articulates visions and allusions that appear throughout the text. At the Drayton, Irene interprets her arrival at the roof top restaurant through fairy-tale references oddly discordant with a hotel that the reader knows to be a segregated facility: "It was, she thought, like being wafted upward on a magic carpet to another world, pleasant, quiet, and strangely remote from the sizzling one that she had left below" (147). In both scenes—the NWA dance and the Drayton—Irene is watching Clare surreptitiously, not as a distant viewer scanning the horizon but with self-protective instincts that require her to be on guard. If we understand the attention *Passing* gives to the written and the racial as being connected, then the electricity between Irene and Clare also evokes the tension between romance and realism, childhood and adulthood, mythmaking and reporting.

In passing for white, Clare Kendry achieved a synthesis that Nella Larsen sought for herself but failed to achieve. Rich, beautiful, widely admired—Clare's identifying characteristics reflect Larsen's own desires. It is little wonder Clare is so often associated with writing, for Larsen ardently wished to establish herself as a professional author. Indeed, it is little wonder that Clare dies at the book's end: the novel's ambivalence toward self-generation parallels Nella Larsen's own struggle for professional stability. The letters between Clare and Irene reflect the novel's attention to aesthetic authenticity, as Gilbert and Gubar have suggested, but the letters between Larsen and Van Vechten problematize their conclusion that for Larsen, "the black female writer inhabits a white world, but longs through her artistry to regain contact with her origins" (153). To the contrary, the evident friendship between Nella Larsen and Carl Van Vechten makes clear that Larsen considered the white world to be part of her origins and that she saw her roots as biracial; moreover, these letters demonstrate her skeptical rebellion against the logic and rhetoric of race loyalty—the very logic, ironically—that shapes much current criticism of Larsen and her work.

Epilogue: Passing in the Present

IN THE FOLLOWING passage from Philip Roth's recent novel *The Human Stain*, the passing protagonist, Coleman Silk, is memorialized by a black colleague:

> Here, in the New England most identified, historically, with the American individualist's resistance to the coercions of a censorious community—Hawthorne, Melville, and Thoreau come to mind—an American individualist who did not think that the weightiest thing in life were the rules, an American individualist who refused to leave unexamined the orthodoxies of the customary and of the established truth, an American individualist who did not always live in compliance with majority standards of decorum and taste—an American individualist *par excellence* was once again so savagely traduced by friends and neighbors that he lived estranged from them until his death, robbed of his moral authority by their moral stupidity. (310–11).

Such specific references make clear that the American literary imagination continues to be enthralled with the relationship between passing and individualism. Coleman Silk understands his decision to pass as a desire for "singularity." He resists the oppressive pull toward racial solidarity that characterized his experience at Howard University. "Overnight the raw I was part of a we with all of the we's overbearing solidity, and he didn't want anything to do with it or with the next oppressive we that came along either," narrator Nathan Zuckerman explains as he struggles to make sense of Silk's life. In *The Human Stain*, appeals to group solidarity and to racial community appear to be little more than tyranny. "You can't let the big they impose its bigotry on you," he realizes, "any more than you can let the little they become a we and impose its ethics on you. . . . Never for him the tyranny of the we that is dying to suck you in, the coercive, inclusive, historical, inescapable moral *we* with its insidious *E pluribus unum*" (108).

In *The Human Stain*, Coleman Silk's world is wrought with irony, and the secret of his true racial origins creates that irony. The most pointed

147

paradox, the novel's central plot line, examines the abrupt and igno-
minious conclusion of Silk's long and distinguished academic career due
to charges of racism. After serving as the powerful and successful dean of
Athena College, after having transformed the dilettantish, aristocratic
faculty into one fitting of a competitive, academically rigorous liberal arts
college, Silk returns to teaching classics prior to what he expects will be a
well-deserved, honorable retirement. But his sense of honor is altered
one day when, in expressing his frustration about the absence of two students who have never once been to class, he asks the class as a whole,
"Does anyone know these people? Do they exist or are they spooks?" That
Silk had no way of knowing the two absentees were African American students who would be deeply offended by what they would consider a racial
insult proved an insufficient defense. The college community turned
against him, shunned him utterly, and Silk became a scapegoat in the
cause of racial sensitivity.

The passer whose success emerged from his utter rejection of community thus felt the full brunt of that same rejection, and it decimated all
of his accomplishments. Seeking support, Silk turns to Herb Keble, an
African American political scientist whom he had hired, but Keble sides
with "them" and explains, "I can't be with you on this, Coleman. I'm going to have to be with them" (16). As Roth makes clear, Keble clearly understands Silk's significance in the conflict between the individual and
the community. It is Keble who memorializes Silk at his funeral. Ostensibly speaking of Silk's estrangement from the Athena College community
in the two years following the "spooks" incident, Keble's resonant sermon
also speaks quite directly of his passing. Roth has given us reason to believe that Keble may well have intuited Silk's secret—he makes clear that
at least one other character in the novel, Silk's thirty-four-year-old lover
Faunia Farley, deduced the truth about Silk early on, and narrator
Nathan Zuckerman realizes it for himself in a moment of shocking insight at the funeral, when he recognizes Silk's sister Ernestine. Whether
or not Keble is speaking of Silk's passing at his funeral, the fact remains
that Silk's insistence on defiant individualism contributed to his failure
as well as his success.

As in the earliest passing fiction, *The Human Stain* points to the family
as a catchall for irreconcilable public and private conflict. Silk's children
grow up believing themselves to be Jewish and are utterly unaware of any
blood relation to black America. Still, in rebelling against what he feels to

be his father's secretive nature (his individualism?), Mark, Coleman Silk's youngest son, embraces Orthodox Judaism. Such a desire for rootedness suggests a longing for connection that countermands the passer's rejection of family, history, and tradition. Likewise, in Danzy Senna's debut novel *Caucasia*, protagonist Birdie Lee wants *not* to pass, wants instead to find and claim her darker sister and to defy her white mother and their white small-town New England life. Like the Ex-Colored Man, who hides his box of fast-yellowing documents as a secret to be protected, Birdie hides her cherished box of "Negrobilia"; like him, she finds in the box and its contents a source of rich connection and familial and cultural comfort; like the Ex-Colored Man, she, too, must change her name, create new identities, travel from place to place. Unlike the Ex-Colored Man, however, Birdie does not want to pass—for her the decision is an obligation, not a choice. In both of these turn of the twenty-first century novels, therefore, we see depictions of a younger generation that renounces the passing of its elders; and we see a longing—even amidst the ironic detachment that characterizes postmodernism—for the sort of integration and community, for example, that Jessie Fauset posited at the end of *Plum Bun*.

This longing is not confined only to contemporary fiction: Shirlee Taylor Haizlip's 1994 memoir *The Sweeter the Juice* details her search for lost relatives who had passed two generations earlier. Some lost family members, like Roth's fictional Mark Silk, had not known about their racial origins. Haizlip's efforts to expose the passing of earlier generations, like Birdie Lee's refusal to live apart from her sister, culminate in her belief that an integrated racial identity offers a far more accurate, far more satisfying, and far more comfortable sense of self than one that accepts the premise of segregation. Haizlip concludes: "All in all, I have grown a great deal less certain about the vagaries of race and know that I am ambivalent about its implications. But I am comfortable with that ambivalence, for it keeps my doors and windows open. It allows me to keep learning. I do not know how I could for so long have failed to understand fully the manipulative nature of the designation 'black' for anyone who had even the fabled 'one drop.' If asked, I would probably now describe myself as a person of mixed race rather than as black, although I know I will never lose my black feelings" (267). Should we read Haizlip's invocation of her "black feelings" as an essentialist challenge to her understanding about the "vagaries of race"? Or would we do better to understand her implicit recognition of segregation logic's artificiality, its potential to misrepresent selfhood as a gesture toward renunciation of that divisive logic? These contemporary texts all seem to strive to undo segregation, even as they articulate its continued resonance a full century after *Plessy v. Ferguson* became law.

Literature will forever be viewed as a medium wherein ethnicity is either celebrated as genuine or exposed as contrived. "In the dynamics of passing," Pamela Caughie observes, "one cannot worry about being exposed as either the real thing or the fraud, for passing contaminates the distinction between the two" (180). The passing figure's white skin does not simply misrepresent his or her racial identity, it also reveals the constructedness of distinctions separating white from black. Danzy Senna, author of *Caucasia,* explains that her novel seeks to expose that construction. "I don't believe in race," she proclaimed in a 1998 interview. "Both blacks and whites have accepted on faith that it's real, but my experience has constantly shown me the absurdity of the whole idea of biological difference" (Vourvoulias B11). And indeed, such a metaphorical understanding of race effectively displaces its real implications and consequences. As Toni Morrison makes clear in her book *Playing in the Dark,* to treat race as a metaphor is to inscribe "blackness" with significance far too charged to be real: "Race has become metaphorical—a way of referring to and distinguishing social forces, events, classes, and expressions of social decay and economic division far more threatening to the body politic than biological 'race' ever was. Expensively kept, economically unsound, a spurious and useless political asset in election campaigns, racism is as healthy today as it was during the Enlightenment. It seems to have a utility far beyond economy, beyond the sequestering of classes from one another, and has assumed a metaphorical life so completely embedded in daily discourse that it is perhaps more necessary and more on display than ever before" (63). The subjugation of race to metaphor renders black Americans and "blackness" itself as objects, mere devices of aesthetic, intellectual, and political inquiry. To be black, Morrison notes, is to serve politicians and to maintain a certain social order: in America, one's skin color makes a political object out of the most apolitical person. When racial differences are thus artificially maintained, the idea of race becomes more important than the appearance of difference. It is precisely the idea of race that passing often critiques in these turn-of-the-century narratives, by complicating the segregationist's definition of white and black.

The apparent intractability of American racism justifiably buttresses all calls for group loyalty. Against this background, however, asserting one's independence and one's sense of individuality proves extremely difficult. Researchers and literary critics are as responsible for this phenomenon as anyone. Henry Louis Gates Jr. makes this clear: "expectations that authors must be accountable spokespersons for their ethnic groups can well nigh be unbearable for an 'ethnic' author. If black authors are primarily entrusted with producing the proverbial 'text of blackness,' they become vulnerable to the charge of betrayal if they shirk their 'duty'" ("Ethnic" 294). To expect that an author act as spokesperson for any single group inevitably necessarily limits that author's artistic complexity. It sustains an artificial distance between racial groups as it facilitates the use of race as a metaphor that is simultaneously supercharged and inhuman. For years, critics have sought a racially loyal agenda from novels about passing and have, as a result, restricted these texts. In fact, many such novels expose the narrow demands of group loyalty, particularly when the group is arbitrarily, if not artificially, defined. The power of the individual, as opposed to the group, to effect change, ought not be underestimated, as Ralph Waldo Emerson's "Self Reliance" so eloquently reminds us. "It is easy in the world to live after the world's opinion; it is easy in solitude to live after our own; but the great man is he who in the midst of the crowd keeps with perfect sweetness the independence of solitude," he proclaims. "We pass for what we are" (23, 25).

Acknowledgments

FOR PERMISSION to reprint previously published and unpublished materials, I am sincerely grateful to the Carl Van Vechten Trust; Carl Van Vechten Papers, Manuscripts and Archives Division, The New York Public Library, Astor, Lenox and Tilden Foundations; and The Yale Collection of American Literature, Beinecke Rare Book and Manuscript Library, Yale University. A version of chapter 3 appeared as "Individualism, Success, and American Identity in *The Autobiography of an Ex-Colored Man*" in *African American Review* 30, no. 3 (1996), and I gratefully acknowledge permission to reuse the material here. A version of chapter 5 appeared as "The Limits of Identity in Jessie Fauset's in *Plum Bun*" in *Legacy* 18, no. 1, and is reprinted by permission of the University of Nebraska Press. Copyright © 2001 by the University of Nebraska Press.

For encouragement, direction, and sound advice during the early stages of this project, I thank Michael T. Gilmore, Wai Chee Dimock, and Werner Sollors. I am especially grateful to Rebecca Morton, Richard Munday, Deborah Tenney, Michael Thurston, Glenn Wallach, and Robert Watson, who read portions of the manuscript and offered support. I have also benefited from the suggestions, queries, and advice of Emily Bernard, Mark Helbling, George Hutchinson, Bruce Kellner, William Maxwell, Adam McKible, Alyssa O'Brien, Tracy Seeley, and Steven Shively. At the University of Massachusetts Press, Clark Dougan provided strong support and helpful encouragement, and Carol Betsch patiently and helpfully guided me through production. Marie Salter wisely and kindly brought order to my prose. The Oakland University community has been supportive in many ways, and I am grateful for two faculty fellowships that funded my research. I have been especially fortunate to join the English department under the wise and calm chairmanship of Brian Connery, whose thoughtful attention to my work deserves special mention. I consider myself blessed with friendly colleagues, scholarly friends, and inspiring students; as this book's dedication makes clear, the English department has welcomed me with more supportive collegiality than I imagined possible. I have also enjoyed the friendship of several distinguished historians, including Sara Chapman, Dan Clark, Karen Miller, and Bruce Zellers. I love my family, and they have influenced me in countless ways; I thank them for keeping my attention focused on the broader implications of scholarly life. My husband, Todd Estes, has read every word of this book at least twice, and I trust that he knows how immeasurably he has helped me as a scholar. He and Elizabeth have been utterly delightful company, and without their companionship in life, I would be very cross indeed.

Works Cited

Abrahams, Roger D. *Deep Down in the Jungle*. Chicago: Aldine, 1970.

Ammons, Elizabeth. "Legacy Profile: Frances Ellen Watkins Harper (1825–1911)." *Legacy* 2 (1985): 61–66.

———. "New Literary History: Edith Wharton and Jessie Redmon Fauset." *College Literature* 14:3 (1987): 207–18.

Andrews, William L. Introduction. *African American Autobiography: A Collection of Critical Essays*. Englewood Cliffs: Prentice, 1993. 1–7.

———. "The Representation of Slavery and Afro-American Literary Realism." *African American Autobiography: A Collection of Critical Essays*. Englewood Cliffs: Prentice, 1993. 77–89.

Ayers, Edward L. *The Promise of the New South: Life After Reconstruction*. New York: Oxford UP, 1992.

Banta, Martha. Introduction. *The Shadow of a Dream and An Imperative Duty*. By William Dean Howells. Ed. Martha Banta. Bloomington: Indiana UP, 1970. iii–xii.

Barnett, Claude A. Letter to Jean Toomer. 23 Apr. 1923. James Weldon Johnson Collection, Beinecke Rare Book and Manuscript Library, Yale, New Haven.

Bell, Bernard. *The Afro-American Novel and Its Tradition*. Amherst: U of Massachusetts P, 1987.

Bennett, Lerone, Jr. *Before the Mayflower*. New York: Penguin, 1988.

Benston, Kimberly W. "I Yam What I Am: The Topos of (Un)naming in Afro-American Literature." *Black Literature and Literary Theory*. Ed. Henry Louis Gates, Jr. New York: Methuen, 1984. 151–72.

Bernard, Emily. "Black Anxiety, White Influence: Carl Van Vechten and the Harlem Renaissance." Diss. Yale U, 1998.

———. *Remember Me to Harlem*. New York: Knopf, 2001.

Berzon, Judith. *Neither White nor Black*. New York: New York UP, 1978.

Birnbaum, Michele. "Racial Hysteria: Female Pathology and Race Politics in Frances Harper's *Iola Leroy* and W. D. Howells's *An Imperative Duty*." *African American Review* 33 (1999): 7–23.

Borus, Daniel H. *Writing Realism: Howells, James, and Norris in the Mass Market*. Chapel Hill: U of North Carolina P, 1989.

Bradley, David. "Looking Behind *Cane*." *The Southern Review* 21 (1985): 682–94.

Browder, Laura. *Slippery Characters*. Chapel Hill: U of North Carolina P, 2000.

Cady, Edwin. *The Realist at War*. Syracuse: Syracuse UP, 1958.

Carby, Hazel. Introduction. *Iola Leroy, or Shadows Uplifted*. By Frances E. W. Harper. Boston: Beacon, 1987.

———. *Reconstructing Womanhood*. New York: Oxford UP, 1987.

Cather, Willa. *A Lost Lady*. New York: Vintage, 1972.

Caughie, Pamela. *Passing and Pedagogy: The Dynamics of Responsibility*. Urbana: U of Illinois, 1999.

Chesnutt, Charles. "The Future American 1: A Complete Race-Amalgamation." *Charles W. Chesnutt: Essays and Speeches*. Ed. Joseph R. McElrath, Jr., Robert C. Leitz, III, and Jesse S. Crisler. Stanford: Stanford UP, 1999. 131–35.

———. "The Future American 3: What the Race Is Likely to Become in the Process of Time." *Charles W. Chesnutt: Essays and Speeches*. Ed. Joseph R. McElrath, Jr., Robert C. Leitz, III, and Jesse S. Crisler. Stanford: Stanford UP, 1999. 121–25.

———. "The Negro in Books." *Charles W. Chesnutt: Essays and Speeches*. Ed. Joseph R. McElrath, Jr., Robert C. Leitz, III, and Jesse S. Crisler. Stanford: Stanford UP, 1999. 426–41.

de Crèvecoeur, J. Hector St. John. *Letters From an American Farmer and Sketches of Eighteenth-Century America*. 1783. New York: Penguin, 1981.

Davis, Thadious M. *Nella Larsen: Novelist of the Harlem Renaissance: A Woman's Life Unveiled*. Baton Rouge: Louisiana State UP, 1994.

Dewey, John. *The Public and Its Problems*. Athens, GA: Swallow, 1988.

Dixon, Thomas. *The Leopard's Spots*. New York: Grossett and Dunlap, 1902.

Douglas, Ann. *Terrible Honesty: Mongrel Manhattan in the 1920s*. New York: Noonday, 1995.

Du Bois, W. E. B. *Black Reconstruction in America 1860–1880*. New York: Touchstone, 1995.

———. "Critiques of Carl Van Vechten's *Nigger Heaven*." *The Portable Harlem Renaissance Reader*. Ed. David Levering Lewis. New York: Viking, 1994. 106–108.

duCille, Ann. *The Coupling Convention*. New York: Oxford UP, 1993.

Dunbar, Paul Laurence. "We Wear the Mask." *Lyrics of Lowly Life*. New York: Dodd, Mead, 1896. 167.

Emerson, Ralph Waldo. *Journals of Ralph Waldo Emerson*. Ed. Edward Waldo Emerson and Waldo Emerson Forbes. Vol. 6. Boston: Houghton, 1909–14.

———. *Self-Reliance and Other Essays*. New York: Dover, 1993.

Ernest, John. "From Mysteries to Histories: Cultural Pedagogy in Frances E. W. Harper's *Iola Leroy*." *American Literature* 64 (1992): 497–518.

Estes-Hicks, Onita. "Jean Toomer and the Politics of National Identity." *Contributions in Black Studies* 7 (1985–86): 22–44.

Fauset, Jessie. Letter to Jean Toomer. 24 Feb. 1922. James Weldon Johnson Collection. Beineke Rare Book and Manuscript Library. Yale U, New Haven.

———. *Plum Bun.* 1928. Boston: Beacon, 1990.

Feeney, Joseph J., S.J. "Black Childhood as Ironic: A Nursery Rhyme Transformed in Jessie Fauset's Novel *Plum Bun.*" *Minority Voices* 4 (1980): 65–69.

———. "A Sardonic, Unconventional Jessie Fauset: The Double Structure and Double Vision of Her Novels." *College Language Association Journal* 22 (1979): 365–82.

Fleming, Robert E. "Irony as a Key to Johnson's *The Autobiography of an Ex-Colored Man.*" *American Literature* 43 (1971): 83–96.

Foner, Eric. *Reconstruction.* New York: Harper, 1988.

Foster, Frances Smith, ed. *A Brighter Coming Day: A Frances Ellen Watkins Harper Reader.* New York: Feminist, 1990.

Frank, Waldo. *Holiday.* New York: Boni and Liveright. 1923.

———. Letters to Jean Toomer. James Weldon Johnson Collection. Beineke Rare Book and Manuscript Library. Yale U, New Haven.

Frederickson, George M. *The Black Image in the White Mind.* New York: Harper, 1971.

Garber, Marjorie. *Vested Interests.* New York: Routledge, 1992.

Garrett, Marvin P. "Early Recollections and Structural Irony in *The Autobiography of an Ex-Colored Man.*" *Critique: Studies in Modern Fiction* 13 (1971): 5–14.

Gates, Henry Louis, Jr. "African American Criticism." *Redrawing the Boundaries.* Ed. Stephen Greenblatt and Giles Gunn. New York: MLA, 1992. 303–19.

———. "'Ethnic and Minority' Studies." *Textual Scholarship.* Ed. Joseph Gibaldi. New York: MLA, 1992. 288–302.

———. *Figures in Black.* New York: Oxford UP, 1987.

———. "Writing, 'Race,' and the Difference It Makes." *Loose Canons.* New York: Oxford UP, 1992. 43–70.

Gilbert, Sandra, and Susan Gubar. *No Man's Land Volume 3: Letters from the Front.* New Haven: Yale UP, 1996.

Gilmore, Michael T. "Hawthorne and the Making of the Middle Class." *Rethinking Class.* Ed. Wai Chee Dimock and Michael T. Gilmore. New York: Columbia UP, 1994. 215–38.

———. "Politics and the Writer's Career: Two Cases." *Reciprocal Influences: Literary Production, Distribution, and Consumption in America.* Ed. Steven Fink and Susan S. Williams. Columbus: Ohio State UP, 1999. 199–212.

Ginsberg, Elaine K. "Introduction: The Politics of Passing." *Passing and the Fictions of Identity.* Durham: Duke UP, 1996. 1–18.

Griffin, Farah Jasmine. *Who Set You Flowin'?* New York: Oxford UP, 1995.

Gubar, Susan. *Racechanges.* New York: Oxford UP, 1997.

Haizlip, Shirlee Taylor. *The Sweeter the Juice.* New York: Simon, 1994.

Hale, Grace Elizabeth. *Making Whiteness.* New York: Pantheon, 1998.

Harper, Frances Ellen Watkins. *Iola Leroy, or Shadows Uplifted.* 1892. Boston: Beacon, 1987.

Harper, Philip Brian. "Fiction and Reform II." *The Columbia History of the American Novel.* Ed. Emory Elliott et. al. New York: Columbia UP, 1991. 216–39.

Hopwood, Avery. Letter to Carl Van Vechten. 22 Sep. 1926. Carl Van Vechten Collection. The New York Public Library.

Howells, William Dean. "Autobiography, a New Form of Literature." *Harper's Monthly* 107 (1909): 795–98.

———. *A Boy's Town.* New York: Harper, 1900.

———. "Criticism and Fiction." *Criticism and Fiction and Other Essays.* Ed. Clara Marburg Kirk and Rudolf Kirk. New York: New York UP, 1959. 9–87.

———. "An Imperative Duty." *Harper's Monthly* 83 (1891): 191–204.

———. *An Imperative Duty.* 1891. The Shadow of a Dream *and* An Imperative Duty. Ed. Edwin H. Cady. New York: Twayne, 1962.

———. Introduction. *Lyrics of Lowly Life.* By Paul Laurence Dunbar. New York: Dodd, Mead, 1896. vii–x.

———. "Mr. Charles W. Chesnutt's Stories." *Atlantic Monthly* 85 (1900): 699–701.

———. "Mrs. Johnson." *Suburban Sketches.* Boston: Houghton, 1884. 11–34.

Hughes, Langston. *The Collected Poems of Langston Hughes.* Ed. Arnold Rampersad. New York: Vintage, 1994.

Hutchinson, George. *The Harlem Renaissance in Black and White.* Cambridge: Belknap, 1995.

———. "Jean Toomer and American Racial Discourse." *Texas Studies in Literature and Language* 35 (1993): 226–50.

———. "Nella Larsen and the Veil of Race." *American Literary History* 9 (1997): 329–49.

Jackson, Miles M., Jr. "Letters to a Friend: Correspondence from James Weldon Johnson to George A. Towns." *Phylon* 29 (1968): 182–98.

Jacobson, Matthew Frye. *Whiteness of a Different Color.* Cambridge: Harvard UP, 1998.

Johnson, James Weldon. *Along This Way.* New York: Penguin, 1990.

———. *The Autobiography of an Ex-Colored Man.* 1912. New York: Penguin, 1990.

Jones, Robert B. *Jean Toomer and the Prison House of Thought.* Amherst: U of Massachusetts P, 1993.

"'Just Americans.'" *Time* 28 Mar. 1932: 19.

Kellner, Bruce. E-mail to the author. 12 Oct. 1999.

Kerman, Cynthia, and Richard Eldridge. *The Lives of Jean Toomer: A Hunger for Wholeness.* Baton Rouge: Louisiana State UP, 1987.

Knopf Publishers. Letters to Jean Toomer. James Weldon Johnson Collection. Beineke Rare Book and Manuscript Library. Yale U, New Haven.

Larsen, Nella [Nella Larsen Imes]. Letters to Carl Van Vechten. 6 Apr. 1927,

3 Mar. 1931, 7 Mar. 1927, 19 Mar. 1928, 5 Oct. 1928. James Weldon Johnson Collection. Beinecke Rare Book and Manuscript Library. Yale U, New Haven.

———. Letters to Carl Van Vechten. 11 Aug. 1926, 6 Oct. 1926. Carl Van Vechten Collection. The New York Public Library.

———. Letter to Dorothy Peterson. n.d. James Weldon Johnson Collection. Beinecke Rare Book and Manuscript Library. Yale U, New Haven.

———. *Passing*. 1929. New York: Penguin, 1997.

Lauter, Paul. "Is Frances Ellen Watkins Harper Good Enough to Teach?" *Legacy* 5 (Spring 1988): 27–34.

Levy, Eugene. *James Weldon Johnson: Black Leader, Black Voice*. Chicago: U of Chicago P, 1973.

Lewis, David Levering. *When Harlem Was in Vogue*. New York: Oxford UP, 1981.

Lippmann, Walter. *Drift and Mastery*. New York: Mitchell Kennerley, 1914.

———. *Public Opinion*. New York: Harcourt, 1922.

Lott, Eric. "Love and Theft: The Racial Unconscious of Blackface Minstrelsy." *Representations* 39 (1992): 23–50.

Lynn, Kenneth. *William Dean Howells: An American Life*. New York: Harcourt, 1970.

McCoy, Beth. "Perpetua(l) Notion: Typography, Economy, and Losing Nella Larsen." *Illuminating Letters*. Ed. Paul C. Gutjahr and Megan L. Benton. Amherst: U of Massachusetts P, 2001. 97–114.

McDowell, Deborah. *"The Changing Same": Black Women's Literature, Criticism, and Theory*. Bloomington: Indiana UP, 1995.

———. "The Neglected Dimensions of Jessie Redmon Fauset." *Afro-Americans in New York Life and History* 5 (1981): 33–49.

Michaels, Walter Benn. "Autobiography of an Ex-White Man: Why Race Is Not a Social Construction." *Transition* 7 (1998): 122–43.

Michie, Helena. *Sororophobia*. New York: Oxford UP, 1992.

Morrison, Toni. *Playing in the Dark*. Cambridge: Harvard UP, 1992.

Myrdal, Gunnar. *An American Dilemma*. New York: Harper, 1962.

O'Sullivan, Maurice J., Jr. "Of Souls and Pottage: James Weldon Johnson's *The Autobiography of an Ex-Colored Man*." *College Language Association Journal* 23 (1979): 60–70.

Perry, Thomas Sergeant. "William Dean Howells." *Century* 23 (1882): 683.

Pisiak, Roxanna. "Irony and Subversion in James Weldon Johnson's *The Autobiography of an Ex-Colored Man*." *Studies in American Fiction* 21 (1993): 83–97.

Porter, Carolyn. *Seeing and Being*. Middletown: Wesleyan UP, 1981.

Rampersad, Arnold. *The Life of Langston Hughes*. Vol. 1. New York: Oxford UP, 1986.

Roediger, David. *The Wages of Whiteness*. New York: Verso, 1991.

Roth, Philip. *The Human Stain*. New York: Houghton, 2000.

Saks, Eva. "Representing Miscegenation Law." *Raritan* 8 (1988): 39–69.

Scruggs, Charles. "The Mark of Cain and the Redemption of Art: A Study of Theme and Structure in Jean Toomer's *Cane*." *American Literature* 44 (1972): 276–91.

Scruggs, Charles, and Lee VanDemarr. *Jean Toomer and the Terrors of American History*. Philadelphia: U of Pennsylvania P, 1998.

Senna, Danzy. *Caucasia*. New York: Riverhead, 1998.

Skerrett, Joseph T., Jr. "Irony and Symbolic Action in James Weldon Johnson's *The Autobiography of an Ex-Colored Man*." *American Quarterly* 32 (1980): 540–58.

Smith, Valerie. *Self-Discovery and Authority in Afro-American Narrative*. Cambridge: Harvard UP, 1987.

Sollors, Werner. *Beyond Ethnicity*. New York: Oxford, 1986.

———. *Neither Black nor White yet Both*. New York: Oxford, 1997.

Somerville, Siobhan B. *Queering the Color Line*. Durham: Duke UP, 2000.

Stevens, Wallace. "Of the Surface of Things." *The Collected Poems*. New York: Vintage, 1982. 57.

Stone, Albert E. "Introduction: American Autobiographies as Individual Stories and Cultural Narrative." *The American Autobiography: A Collection of Critical Essays*. Ed. Albert E. Stone. Englewood Cliffs: Prentice, 1981. 1–9.

Stowe, Harriet Beecher. *A Key to Uncle Tom's Cabin*. Boston: John P. Jewett, 1853.

———. *Uncle Tom's Cabin*. New York: Penguin, 1982.

Sundquist, Eric. *To Wake the Nations*. Cambridge: Harvard UP, 1993.

Sylvander, Carolyn Wedin. *Jessie Redmon Fauset: Black American Writer*. Troy: Whitston, 1981.

Tate, Claudia. *Domestic Allegories of Political Desire*. New York: Oxford UP, 1992.

———. "Nella Larsen's *Passing*: A Problem of Interpretation." *Black American Literature Forum* 14 (1980): 142–46.

Toll, Robert C. *Blacking Up*. New York: Oxford UP, 1974.

Tompkins, Jane. *Sensational Designs*. New York: Oxford UP, 1985.

Tonnies, Ferdinand. *Community and Society*. 1957. Trans. and Ed. Charles P. Loomis: East Lansing: Michigan State UP. 1964.

Toomer, Jean. *Cane*. 1923. New York: Liveright, 1993.

———. "The Crock of Problems." *Jean Toomer: Selected Essays and Literary Criticism*. Ed. Robert B. Jones. Knoxville: U of Tennessee P, 1996. 55–59.

———. "The Hill." *Jean Toomer: Selected Essays and Literary Criticism*. Ed. Robert B. Jones. Knoxville: U of Tennessee P, 1996. 92–98.

———. Letter to Horace Liveright. 5 Sept. 1923. James Weldon Johnson Collection. Beinecke Rare Book and Manuscript Library. Yale U, New Haven.

———. "Opinions on the Questions of the *Cahiers de l'Etoile*." *Jean Toomer: Selected*

Essays and Literary Criticism. Ed. Robert B. Jones. Knoxville: U of Tennessee P, 1996. 86–91.

———. "Outline of the Story of the Autobiography." Unpublished typescript. James Weldon Johnson Collection. Beineke Rare Book and Manuscript Library. Yale U, New Haven.

———. "'The Second River' or 'From Exile into Being.'" Unpublished typescript. James Weldon Johnson Collection. Beineke Rare Book and Manuscript Library. Yale U, New Haven.

———. "The South in Literature." *Jean Toomer: Selected Essays and Literary Criticism.* Ed. Robert B. Jones. Knoxville: U of Tennessee P, 1996. 11–16.

Trachtenberg, Alan. Preface. *The Memoirs of Waldo Frank.* Amherst: U of Massachusetts P, 1973.

Turner, Darwin T. *The Wayward and the Seeking.* Washington: Howard UP, 1980.

Twain, Mark. *Pudd'nhead Wilson.* New York: Signet, 1980.

Van Vechten, Carl. "The Negro in Art: How Shall He Be Portrayed?" *The Crisis* 32 (March 1926): 219.

———. *Nigger Heaven.* 1926. Introd. Kathleen Pfeiffer. Urbana: U of Illinois P, 2000.

———. Typescript of interview by William Ingersoll for the Oral History Collection, Columbia U. 3 Mar. 1960.

Vourvoulias, Bill. "Talking with Danzy Senna: Invisible Woman." *Newsday* 29 Mar. 1998: B11.

Wald, Gayle. *Crossing the Line.* Durham: Duke UP, 2000.

Walker, Alice. "The Divided Life of Jean Toomer." *In Search of Our Mother's Gardens.* New York: Harcourt, 1983. 60–65.

Wall, Cheryl. *Women of the Harlem Renaissance.* Bloomington: Indiana UP, 1995.

Warren, Kenneth. *Black and White Strangers.* Chicago: U of Chicago P, 1993.

———. "Possessing the Common Ground: William Dean Howells's *An Imperative Duty.*" *American Literary Realism* 20 (1988): 23–37.

Washington, Booker T. *Up from Slavery.* New York: Doubleday, 1963.

Watson, Steven. *The Harlem Renaissance.* New York: Pantheon, 1995.

Weinberg, Jonathan. "'Boy Crazy': Carl Van Vechten's Queer Collection." *The Yale Journal of Criticism* 7 (1994): 25–49.

Whyde, Janet. "Mediating Forms: Narrating the Body in Jean Toomer's *Cane.*" *Southern Literature* 26 (1993): 42–53.

Williamson, Joel. *The Crucible of Race.* New York: Oxford UP, 1984.

Wonham, Henry B. "Writing Realism, Policing Consciousness: Howells and the Black Body." *American Literature* 67 (1995): 701–24.

Woodward, C. Vann. *The Strange Career of Jim Crow.* New York: Oxford UP, 1996.

Zangrando, Robert L. "Lynching." *The Reader's Companion to American History.* Ed. Eric Foner and John A. Garraty. Boston: Houghton, 1991. 684–86.

Index

Kathleen Pfeiffer is associate professor of English at Oakland University in Rochester, Michigan, where she teaches American and African American literature.